BIG IDEAS
FOR LITTLE BUDGETS

John Bytheway

Brad Wilcox

ISBN: 1-55517-078-1

Typesetting and design by Prime Music Engraving, Orem UT
Printed in the United States of America
Second Printing; July 1994
Third Printing; July 1995

To our great example and wonderful friend,
David Alma Christensen

For possible future volumes,

SEND YOUR IDEAS
to

John Bytheway and Brad Wilcox
2311 South 1700 East
Salt Lake City, Utah 84106

"The human mind,
once stretched by a
new idea,
never regains its
original dimensions."

–Oliver Wendall Holmes
Utah Endowment for the Humanities
1989 Report to the People

Table of Contents

Acknowledgments

We express appreciation to all those who so willingly shared their wonderful ideas with us. We thank our parents, Jack and Diane Bytheway and Ray and Val Wilcox for their support. We also acknowledge Brad's wife, Debi, and all our brothers and sisters for their help and encouragement.

We are grateful to John Perry for his professional help and to Craig Bradley, Ron Hills and Glen McClure for getting us together. Thanks as well, and as always, to Chloe Vroman, Beth Duering, and George Bickerstaff.

It has been said that ideas are like children—your own are wonderful. To the best of our knowledge, throughout the book, we have given credit to the originator of the idea. However, we realize that some ideas are re-tellings of successful activities someone has seen. In such cases, we have credited the one who first submitted the idea to us though we know they alone may not be responsible for it.

Foreword

Compiled in this book are creative, low-cost, and faith-building ideas submitted by Latter-day Saints across the United States, Canada and various other countries. We share their ideas, along with many of our own, in hopes of providing something that everyone can adopt and adapt to fit their own unique needs.

These are not detailed, step-by-step instructions or just-add-people-and-stir recipes. Rather, it is our hope that the ideas compiled here will be a spring-board from which all of us can jump to higher levels of creativity and spirituality.

When explaining the budget program of the Church, Elder Boyd K. Packer stated, "There will still be many activities . . . [however,] they will be scaled down in both time and money" (*Ensign*, May, 1990, p.90). It is our hope that this book will provide some practical suggestions for such scaling down. We hope the ideas presented here will help us adjust and cut back without losing the spiritual, testimony-building, service oriented, family and fun flavors that have always been staple items on LDS menus.

It is as though we are being wisely counseled to follow a carefully planned, well-balanced diet. We all agree that it is healthy to trim needless sugar and fat from our meals. Those who look at the budget as an endless fast are probably going to the extreme.

In addition to ideas on inexpensive ward and family activities, this book offers low-cost and group-involving ideas for decorations, refreshments, and dances. We do not mean to imply that decorations, refreshments and dances are essential or necessary. That would depend on what you hope to acheive. If the main goal of an upcoming activity is to create an opportunity for a spiritual experience, nice decorations would likely rank low in importance. On an airplane trip, one can forego the peanuts, soft drinks, nice interior and extra leg-room. The main goal is to get where you're going. Imagine how upset someone would be, even if they flew first class with all the extras, if the pilot took them to the wrong destination!

Elder Gordon B. Hinckley has stated that we are "people of ingenuity who with faith and prayer can work out programs costing little in dollars that will yield tremendous dividends in wholesome recreation and faith-building activities" (*Ensign*, May, 1990 p.97). Our destination is clear. If this compilation can be a useful tool for reaching the ends so clearly specified by our prophet leaders, our efforts will have been worthwhile.

1 FORECAST: BRAINSTORMING

When the announcement of the new Church budget was made, many were tempted to predict a future of dark, cloudy skies and endless rain. Now there are other ways to view the weather. Many of us are seeing storms—but not the same kind originally predicted by so many. The storms of the present and the storms on the horizon are not rain storms, but brainstorms.

For many, the new Church budget program has presented a challenge. Brainstorming can be a positive way to meet that challenge. When working with groups, presidencies, or committees, here are some basic steps to keep in mind:

PRAY American author Christian Nestell Bovee once said, "A great thought is a great boon, for which God is to be first thanked" (Tyron Edwards, ed. *The New Dictionary of Thoughts*, rev. ed. [New York: Hanover House, 1960] p.i.). Our creative friend, Shaaron Saunders from Ohio, was once at a conference where one of the presenters used an idea that she had first developed. When the presenter gave no credit to Shaaron, she could have become a little upset. Instead, Shaaron said, "I believe in giving credit where credit is due. However, if you trace all bright ideas back to their true source, they all come from God."

In the process of brainstorming, as with anything we do, prayer is a vital first and continuing step. Under the Church budget program, many decisions about details are being left to local leaders and members of the Church. With that responsibility comes a greater need for personal revelation. Elder Packer promises, "You will become more dependent upon the Spirit" (*Ensign*, May 1990, p.89). We must open and continue that spiritual communication through prayer.

> But behold, I say unto you
> that ye must pray always . . .
> that ye must not perform any
> thing unto the Lord save in
> the first place ye shall
> pray unto the Father in the
> name of Christ, that he will
> consecrate thy performance unto
> thee, that thy performance
> may be for the welfare of thy
> soul (2 Nephi 32:8).

PLAN Begin with your purpose and objective clearly before you. Beginning with the end in mind keeps us from getting so caught up planning the trip that we forget where we are going.

It helps to actually write your destination or objective out. It can be as simple as, "We have to plan a ward dinner," or it can be more detailed, like, "We must plan a ward activity that will involve the youth, bring out the less-active and make the new bishopric more available and approachable."

PREPARE If it is a brainstorm you are after, you can increase your chances of getting one if you seed the clouds a bit. Make special invitations to the meeting where you will be planning. Tell those who are invited the purpose of the meeting in advance. They will likely arrive better prepared.

When dealing with young people, it is wise to have them represented in some way. The year before Brad's mission, he had the opportunity to serve as the only youth representative on the National Executive Board of the Boy Scouts of America. He was working with remarkable men—presidents of large companies and corporations—who were making important decisions about the future of the Scouting program.

In one meeting, they were discussing why scouts would not wear the pants of the scout uniform. They debated long and loud about the cost of the pants and whether they were comfortable. Finally, the chairman said, "Brad, you're our youth representative, why won't the scouts wear the pants?" Everyone turned and looked at Brad. Presidents of national and international corporations were listening to an eighteen year old.

Brad cleared his throat and said, "It has nothing to do with comfort or cost, it's just that the pants look really geeky. They're not cool." Light bulbs went on. Heads nodded. Assignments were made. The men in that meeting were glad a young person had been given a chance to express his views. Brad still smiles to himself when he sees the new uniforms—more fashionable, more athletic looking and, definitely, more "cool."

PRODUCE Someone should be a scribe so that all ideas—no matter how crazy—can be recorded. Start by clearly stating your purpose and reviewing some basics rules of cooperation and courtesy, if needed. Then, prime the pump by sharing some ideas that you have come up with. Beginning with, "So, who has an idea?" is as awkward as an uncertain teenage boy picking up his date and saying, "What shall we do now?" Get the ball rolling first. Then throw it out to the group.

Some might say, "I can't think of anything new. I just can't come up with anything original." Remind them that originality is only part of creativity. Most definitions of the word also include flexibility and fluency as well.

The term, "synthesis" refers to taking many parts from different places and creating a new whole. Latter-day Saints have a unique understanding of this concept for we have been taught that even the creation of the world itself was an act of organizing matter that was already there (Moses 2).

An idea does not need to be new to be original. We like the way Thomas Wentworth Higginson put it: "Originality is simply a pair of fresh eyes" (Edwards, p.459). Car designers do not re-invent the wheel every year. They simply add a new color or stripe to the car. Cooks do not re-invent vegetables. They put them in a new sauce. You do not have to be very old to realize that the fashions that people pay big money for today are simply re-makes of what your parents wore in high school. Rather than worrying so much about creating something new, focus more on accomplishing your purpose. It is said that industry is a better horse to ride than genius.

PRAISE Once the brainstorm starts and ideas begin to pour, reinforce those you are with by complimenting and building them. Withhold critical comments on the ideas for now. When you finally start getting the idea rain for which you have prayed, it is not time to evaluate it—just start singing in it. Brainstorms last longer and are better in positive and lifting environments. As people begin running dry of ideas, thank them for participating and praise their efforts. Review the entire list that has been recorded by the scribe. You'll find that silly or impractical ideas will naturally start dying without anyone having to point them out or give them a funeral.

POLISH Once you have settled on a few good ideas, begin the brainstorming process all over again, pin-pointing those ideas specifically. Ask questions: How can these activities be expanded to include more people? How can they be done at least cost? How can these activities be made to be more spiritual? Fine-tune selected ideas until they meet your purpose.

PROCEED Make assignments. If something needs looking into to see if it's a realistic possibility, assign someone to do the looking. Delegate responsibilities immediately while everyone is still wet with the excitement of the storm.

So what is the forecast for the future? If we see storms, let them be brainstorms. As we learn to pray, plan, prepare, produce, praise, polish and proceed, we will positively be in position to proclaim, "Please, let it pour!"

2 FENCES, COWS & ATTITUDES

An effective analogy about standards refers to cows—not eight-cow dates for Johnny Lingo—but rather, cows inside of fences. Les Johnson has written about his boyhood memories of cows on his farm. He remembers watching them in the pasture and noting that, while most of them grazed contentedly, a few could always be found pushing against the fence ("Looking For a Fence." *Scouting*, December, 1964, pp.14-15).

When it comes to LDS standards, definite fences have been erected. The caution offered to young people is to be careful that they do not become so busy pushing against those fences that they overlook the spacious pasture and delicious, green grass that lie within.

Like Church standards, the Church budget program provides fences for all members of the Church. Elder Packer assures, "The [budget] change will require a considerable adjustment in our thinking" (*Ensign*, May 1990, p.89). There are six attitudes we can foster that will help us with that adjustment:

A POSITIVE ATTITUDE

In Chile, where Brad served his mission, there are seasons of the year when the rain seems endless. During one such soggy time, the mission president looked gloomily out of his window thinking of the hardship and inconvenience the heavy rain was for his missionaries.

Just then, his little daughter came bouncing into the room. "Oh Daddy!" she exclaimed. "Isn't the rain wonderful? Now, no one will want to go outside so everyone will be at home when the missionaries knock at their doors."

Benjamin Franklin said, "The discontented man finds no easy chair" (*Reader's Digest*, April 1990, p.51). By the same token, the contented man can make many an uncomfortable arrangement easy by being positive.

A GRATEFUL ATTITUDE

President Hinckley has said, "I am thankful that the day has come, at last, when for the Latter-day Saints in the United States and Canada, the payment of honest tithes and generous offerings will provide the means for facilities and activities whereby we may worship together, learn together and socialize together . . . Be grateful" (*Ensign*, May 1990, p.95). We don't usually think of singing the hymn, "Count your many blessings . . ." when we receive less of something. However, in this case, less can mean a great deal more to us than we think.

Elder Packer promises, "Nothing essential will be lost, rather essentials will be rediscovered, be found!" (*Ensign*, May 1990, p.89). The hymn promises, "Count your blessings. Name them one by one. And it will surprise you what the Lord has done." (*Hymns*, #241). The Church budget program has already left many surprised. But it has been a nice surprise. Now, it is time to count the blessings—one by one.

A FRUGAL ATTITUDE

Brad's grandmother, Mary Camenish, was an excellent example of frugality. He shares the following:

> Unlike many of my friends, whose grandmothers lived whole continents away, my Grandma always lived right in my same ward. Our family always sat together in Sacrament Meeting, and somehow, it seemed I always ended up next to Grandma.
>
> "Hold it right there," Grandma whispered. My mind was wandering to a burst of Sunday morning light through the chapel window. No doubt I was thinking of rolling down the sloping church lawn outside.
>
> "Hold it steady, Brad." I readjusted the tattered hymn book and peeled it open on

Grandma's knee. She dipped into her file-cabinet purse and brought out the mending kit. Carefully she broke off a strip of tape and placed it along a badly torn page, patting it down securely. We were an unlikely repair crew; Grandma was seventy, I was seven. But every weekend, dressed in Sunday best, there we were.

She flipped the page over to tape the other side. "Ere You Left Your Room This Morning" was the name of the hymn, but someone had taken creative license, and it now read, "Did you air your room this morning, did you think to spray?" I smiled. Grandma shook her head. As soon as the tape was in place, her busy fingers pulled out the art gum eraser, and she handed it to me. I rubbed out the scribbles and brushed away all evidence of the tampering. We went on, page after page, through the old hymnal. We worked quietly, of course, never repairing beyond the book rack immediately in front of us. But every Sunday, wherever we sat, there were always tattered books that needed the mending kit, Grandma's patience, and me.

Chances are that at least once during all my childhood church meetings someone stood at the pulpit to eloquently admonish me to take care of the Lord's house and respect Church property—to be industrious and frugal. Surely, at least once, someone must have given a soul-stirring address on the matter. But I really can't recall, for the most memorable Sacrament Meeting lectures I received were the silent ones Grandma gave to me every Sunday.

Speaking about the Church budget program, President Gordon B. Hinckley said, "We know that we are accountable to the Lord for the stewardship given us. We must be prudent. We must be conservative. We must be careful" (*Ensign*, May 1990, p.96). We now have the opportunity to practice the same kind of frugality taught by Brad's Grandma.

A CREATIVE ATTITUDE

Elder Thomas S. Monson has stated, "The ingenuity of our people is well known" (*Ensign*, May

1990, p.97). Most definitely, ingenuity and creativity are part of our LDS heritage.

In 1919, a devoted convert to the Church named Harry Hale Russell was doing extensive family history research and temple work for his departed ancestors in the Salt Lake Temple. His wife, Dolly McEntire Russell, recorded, "At a time when we could do only one endowment a day, you can see what an effort it was for the two of us to complete 360 names—papa with his heart and me with arthritis in my knees. About that time, we heard of possible relatives living in southern Utah and planned a visit. We found them all right—and we found they had been doing the same names from the very same book in the St. George Temple!"

Brother Russell was discouraged to discover that both families had spent literally years duplicating each others efforts. He said, "If this could happen in two temples, it could be happening in all seven." That very day, Harry Hale Russell determined that he would develop a way to insure that there would never be a chance of such wasteful duplication again. It meant years of struggle and sacrifice for the Russell family, but Harry's inspired work was the beginning of the Temple Index Bureau. After its establishment, duplications avoided during the first few years alone amounted to almost six million (*The Utah Genealogical and Historical Magazine*, April 1936, pp.82-83; Personal History of Dolly Elizabeth McEntire Russell).

Harry Russell's contribution blessed members of the Church throughout history and on both sides of the veil. Our purposes might not be so grand or far reaching. However, each assignment we carry out, activity we plan and calling we magnify is important and worthwhile.

An ancient Japanese proverb that states, "If you simply deal with the problem, the problem becomes simple." The Church budget program is a call for the creative problem solvers of our day to come forth.

AN OBEDIENT ATTITUDE

"Look beyond the narrow boundaries of your own wards," counsels President Hinckley, "and rise to the larger vision of this the work of God . . . I remind you that we should recognize that this Church is not a social club. This is the kingdom of God on earth" (*Ensign*, May 1990, p.97).

A SACRIFICING ATTITUDE

President N. Eldon Tanner once wrote, "Sacrifice means going without or giving up something which is good for something which is better" (*MTC Gospel Study Lessons*, 1981, p.2). When early Saints gave up their established city of Nauvoo to follow a Prophet to the West, they gave up something good indeed. Was the arid Utah desert better? They had to make it better. And we now, like cows in a pasture, could end up longing for the green hills of overly extravagant, super activities that lie outside the fence unless we take advantage of our present meadow.

Developing attitudes which are positive, grateful, frugal, creative, obedient, and sacrificing will place us right in the center of the greenest pasture we can imagine. The scriptures even promise, "and in Him they shall find pasture" (1 Nephi 22:25). As with the cows, if we will stop pushing against the fence, we might be able to see the potential banquet waiting all around us.

ADAPTABLE TO WARD, STAKE, YOUTH, PRIMARY, QUORUM

ACADEMY AWARDS

Have the different units or groups you are working with prepare an original script around a theme, much like a road show. Videotape the productions and show them (excerpts if they are too long) on "Academy Awards" night. The evening may be formal and include awards for most creative, most humorous, biggest production, etc.

—Ron and Rhonda Reily, Orange, California

ARTS AND CRAFTS SHOWCASE

Plan the activity well in advance so that everyone will have time to prepare. Members of your group display their art, crafts or photography. Have workshops preparing for this event with instruction and presentations from local artists or allow everyone to prepare on their own.

Variations: *A fun variation (especially for those who are reluctant to share before their peers) is to arrange with mothers to get a picture that was drawn by every member of your group when they were very young. Frame the picture (or a copy of the picture) with black paper or mat board. During the evening, participants can guess the artists before the names are officially unveiled.*

LIP SYNCS

Most people feel awkward or embarrassed performing a serious talent or singing a song before their peers, but almost everyone will be willing to participate in a Lip Sync. You can provide the songs and a short amount of time for each group to prepare or you can simply make assignments. Sometimes, it is successful to work around a theme such as show tunes, fifties songs, or any song that mentions a particular word. Actions and costumes add to the fun. Shorten songs or simply use one verse and chorus of a long song to keep things moving.

—Becky Crockett, Phoenix, Arizona; Clark Smith, Mountain View, California

Variations: *Use props for instruments (tennis racket for a guitar, etc.) Video the performances to view later or simply project what the video camera is picking up live onto a large screen while it is happening on stage.*

MINUTE MELODRAMAS

Producing a melodrama that is already written is fun to do, but takes a lot of time and effort. It is just as fun to make some up in a minute. Divide the participants into small groups. Give them a basic plot (the villain is going to kick the young widow out of her home. The hero saves the day and falls in love with the widow). Every member is involved in a main part or simply as a prop (swinging doors, trees, children, pets, etc.). Groups are all given a time limit to gather what costumes they can and practice. All groups then report back and perform for each other complete with cheers for the hero, boos for the villain and popcorn for everyone. Video cameras can add to the fun.

—Robin Gunnell, Mary Lois Gunnell, Orem, Utah

Variations: *Use fairy tales, stories from Church history, scripture stories, or nursery rhymes.*

ACT OUT SCRIPTURE STORIES

Assign groups a story from the scriptures they can prepare to act out before the group. It's easiest to use a narrator to read or tell the story rather than having lines to remember. Costumes may be minimal.

—Robin Gunnell, Debbie Hawkins, Orem, Utah; Lucile Carter, Provo, Utah

Variations: *With older groups, stories could be presented in a new setting or period in history. Nephi could be commanded to build an airplane or a modern Lehi commanded to leave his home and not take his VCR, CD player or Microwave. Video cameras to record the event will increase the excitement.*

SKITS IN A BAG

Present each group with a garbage bag full of miscellaneous props. They are given a time limit in which to prepare a skit using each of the props provided.

Variations: *They must follow a Church theme or the theme of the conference. Everyone could follow the same basic story or script and work in their different props.*

READER'S THEATER

While actually producing a play is costly and time consuming, gathering to simply read the play is relatively easy and satisfying to both performers and audience. Provide copies of the script and assign parts. Once through could be the end of the fun or you could choose to practice it several times and present the reading to an audience.

(Tips from *The Activity Book*, LDS, 1977, pp.69-70: Readers theater is usually performed with little emphasis on movement, costumes, props, or scenery. It is up to the readers (with scripts in hand) to create the action and setting in the imagination of the audience. Choose or write a script, prepare a narrative to introduce the production and provide for transitions.)

VARIETY SHOW

Focus on the talents of participants and put together a showcase of variety and entertainment.

(Tips from *The Activity Book*, LDS, 1977. p.70: Plan the program to involve many but don't try to include too many acts in one show. An hour program is long enough. Choose a good master of ceremonies who can keep the show running smoothly between acts. Make sure all sound, lighting and other stage equipment work properly. Perhaps you can present your program as a service project at a rest home.)

GETTING TO KNOW YOUR BISHOP

Plan a surprise social activity to honor the bishop. Meet with the bishop's wife to coordinate the activity and get information about the bishop's life. Possible activities would be to invite friends of the bishop to share their memories of him, or have different members of your group assigned to report on different aspects of his life. Display pictures and mementos of his life along with a chart of his Priesthood line of authority. Let the members of your group express appreciation to the bishop. Honor as many of his family who can come as well.

—*The Activity Book*, LDS, 1977, p.152

Variations: *Use the same idea for the Relief Society President, stake leaders, scout master, leaders of any given organization, focus on individual members or group one-at-a-time.*

GUESS WHO NIGHT

Have each member of your group bring to this activity a picture of himself as a baby or young child. Assign each picture a number and display the pictures throughout the room. Give each person a paper and pencil and have them identify the person in the pictures. It can add fun if everyone will try to come up with the most clever caption for each picture as well. Vote on the favorite. As pictures are identified, have the person in the picture tell one of his earliest of favorite childhood memories.

—*The Activity Book*, LDS, 1977, p.152

Variations: *Play the same game using baby clothes, clothes still in the closet from past eras and fashions, or something else from their past (high school trophies, ribbons, letters, etc.).*

GETTING TO KNOW YOU

Everyone lists anonymously on a sheet of paper answers to questions about favorite subjects, games and activities, books, vacations, foods, desserts, and other items. Shuffle the sheets and have a lively time matching them with the people who wrote them.

—*Sharla Luker, Salt Lake City, Utah,* Ensign, *March, 1982, p.49*

Variations: *By the information on the sheets, match people to be partners or companions for a game or for the evening. Have people write something that happened to them as a child that few people know about or a nice thing that they have done that no one knows about.*

BOOK SWAP

Have a neighborhood or ward book swap. Children bring anything from comic books to classics and adults trade paperbacks, recipe or Church books. Trades can be for long enough to read the books or more permanent.

—*Sharla Luker, Salt Lake City, Utah,* Ensign, *July, 1981, p.53*

Variations: *Swap board games, clothes, toys, tapes, family videos.*

ASSEMBLE GROUP BOOKLETS

By having every member of your group contribute one item, booklets can be compiled for a variety of purposes. Cookbooks are commonly done this way with everyone providing a favorite recipe. Using the same idea, compile a booklet of family holiday traditions or a booklet of favorite holiday poems or stories. Ask everyone to bring stories or quotes centered on a particular Gospel topic or theme. Cut the cost involved by having everyone bring copies of their own offering. Set all these stacks around a room and have each person compile their own booklet by taking one of each stack.

—*Rand Packer, Provo, Utah*

Variations: *Assemble books of quotes, thoughts, favorite talks or articles out of Church magazines, stories that have been written by the individuals themselves.*

TEACHING SOMETHING NEW

Have participants teach each other something they're good at. For example, have someone teach how to bake bread and then another teach how to change tires. Everyone has the chance to shine by teaching something that they do well.

Variations: *Learn a skill as a group and then teach it to a younger group, or teach in another class or ward. Assign each person a topic that everyone is interested in. Have them prepare on their own and report back to teach the group.*

★ SURPRISE BREAKFAST

Surprise a member of your class or quorum early in the morning with a breakfast in bed! Or make them wear the funniest things you can find in their closet and take them out to breakfast.

Variations: *Do the same thing with lunches, dinners, snacks, meet at someone's home or at the Church rather than going out.*

★ COUNT BLESSINGS

Sometimes we feel a bit overwhelmed with everything that we are expected to do in a day as Latter-day Saints. Focus, as well, on all the latter-day blessings we have been given so we can devote more time to the mission of the Church and less time to simply feeding and clothing ourselves. Divide into teams and have each team responsible to list or label all the time-saving devises they can. Examples would be toasters, freezers, cars, telephones, tractors, dishwashers, etc.

—Helen Free VanderBeck, Idaho Falls, Idaho, Ensign, *March, 1981, p.34*

Variations: *Count time-saving devices by finding their pictures in magazines, creating a cross word puzzle, or a word-find puzzle. Cut the different pictures up and create a jigsaw puzzle, or draw pictures, in a "pictionary"-type game.*

★ CAREER SEARCH AND CLINIC

Arrange for specialists, or have participants come with information they have prepared on different careers. Have them speak to the group and answer questions. Groups may rotate and have displays and exhibits on the different careers.

—The Activity Book, LDS, 1977, pp.35-36

Variations: *Have presentations on other interests, Gospel topics of study, talents, Questions about Church history or doctrine.*

HOBBY SHOW

Invite participants to set up a display of hobbies. Hobby specialists could come and share and demonstrate music, writing, sports, stamp collecting, etc. You could discuss how hobbies can provide enjoyment, enrichment, supplemental income or lead to careers.

—*The Activity Book*, LDS, 1977, p.36

ANYTIME CAROLING

Go "caroling" to someone's home during any time of year and sing any kind of songs.

Variations: *Go anytime trick-or-treating, anytime valentines, or go to the airport and welcome a total stranger off the plane with horns and banners.*

CHORAL FESTIVAL

Each Ward Choir or designated organization can prepare a number to present. One song from each ward will fill an evening. On a smaller scale, each organization from a ward or each class or quorum from YM/YW or primary can prepare a number to present in a mini festival. Choose a familiar song that all can sing together as a finale to the activity.

Variations: *Hold a festival for dance or speech (prepared or impromptu and extemporaneous* —The Activity Book, *LDS, 1977, pp.57-58) or a festical about foreign countries, storytelling, scenes from the scriptures or Church history, or write your own program using hymns or the Children's Song Book. Do a program using LDS choral music.*

WRITING OR ART CONTEST

This can be done on a volunteer basis, or, bring out hidden talents by encouraging all to participate. Provide different categories such as poetry, short story, personal experience, etc. in writing. Establish rules and select qualified judges. Prizewinners can be published in ward newspapers and all can be encouraged to enter contests provided by the Church Magazines.

—Val C. Wilcox, Provo, Utah

COLLECTIONS

Set out to get the most leaves, rocks, sticks, etc. You can even do something with them when you return: Make collages or rock people with glue and paint.

Variations: *Gather different color squares of tissue paper, garbage, pop cans, etc.*

COOKING OR DECORATING CONTEST

Have a good, old-fashioned cooking, baking or cake decorating contest. Restrictions on who can help make it more challenging. Taste the products and share recipes.

—The Activity Book, LDS, 1977, p.28

Variations: *Contests with jello molds, pancake flipping, pancakes in shapes or characters—Mouse with ears.*

INTERNATIONAL COOKING

Invite each participant to prepare a food item from another country. Have them tell something about the country where the food originated and then sample the foods. Exchange recipes.

—The Activity Book, LDS, 1977, p.28

Variations: *Dress from the country, guess the country, guess the ingredients in the food, display, draw, or color flags from each country.*

NEW FOOD PARTY

Have people assigned to bring fruits or vegetables that others are unlikely to have tried. Set up some taster tables and the motto, "Try it, you might like it."

—Lori Kraykovic, Idaho Falls, Idaho, Ensign, *March, 1978, p.56*

EARN YOUR DINNER

Decide on a goal, hours of service, scripture reading, reading the Church Magazines and have participants earn parts of a dinner by completing the goal. A certain number of chapters equals your beverage or salad. More chapters equal your main course. Have participants earn each of their utensils and plates. At the end of a given time limit, gather for a pot luck at the Church or at a leader's home where everyone gets exactly what he or she earned.

—Debi Wilcox, Georgia Rassmusen, Provo, Utah

Variations: *Earn your sundae, tacos, banana splits, ingredients in a batch of chocolate chip cookies (flour, sugar, chips, etc.).*

FASHION SHOW

This activity can be a traditional fashion show. Contact stores and arrange to use some of the latest clothes (many will do this at no cost because of the advertising benefits). Members can also model things they make themselves, Sunday clothes or pajamas. The activity can be formal or casual.

—*The Activity Book*, LDS, 1977, p.154

Variations: *Really stretch the idea by having people model what they can do with garbage sacks, Halloween costumes, baby bibs, or "ugly" fashions—something you wouldn't be caught dead in.*

SIMULATED AIRPLANE FLIGHT ACTIVITY

Arrange the cultural hall like the inside of an airliner without informing participants of the plans for the evening. Give them all airline tickets and inform them that they are all going on a trip. You can be really creative with sound effects and flight attendants, etc. Partway through the flight all the lights go out and a person in white appears before the crowd informing them that they have all died in a crash. The person in white tells them that he has been given special permission to give them a tour of all the kingdoms. Using the scriptures, have the angel accompany the group to different rooms representing Spirit Prison, the Telestial and Terrestrial kingdoms, and describe the places and the lives and works of those who will inhabit them. The final stop of the tour is in the Celestial Kingdom where the participants will find relatives and leaders in the choir seats dressed in white. The activity ends with a testimony meeting.

HIJACKED DINNER

Advertize that your dinner will follow a certain theme (Hawaiian, for example). Have everyone dress accordingly. As they arrive, have them board a plane (the overflow area of the chapel arranged like the seats on an airplane) where they receive a small appetizer. Then have some people set up to hijack the plane to somewhere else, like Mexico. They can really ham it up and finally open the doors into the cultural hall. It can be decorated with things from Mexico and everyone can enjoy a Mexican meal of stack tacos or something similar.

—*Carole Crockett, Phoenix, Arizona;*

Variations: *Try setting things up like a cruise on a ship.*

GAME SHOW SPIN-OFFS

Plan an activity around a favorite TV game show like "Family Feud." Personalize the rules and or questions to fit the needs of your group. For example, "Name something on the Bishop's desk, name a Temple with Moroni on top, name a family in our ward that keeps a great garden." Adapt the same rules they use on T.V.

Variations: *Select several couples to answer questions for you version of the "Newlywed Game." (How often will your spouse say he/she reads the* Ensign *magazine?) Singles could play the dating game where a sister has to choose between three mystery bachelors who must disguise their voices. Play "Wheel of Fortune" and have the hidden words be Church-related nouns or personalized words about your group (people's middle names or birthdays), or try Name That Hymn (in how few notes are you able to recognize the Church Hymns and Primary songs?), or take a favorite character from the scriptures or church history and play "What's My Line?"*

GOSPEL TREASURE HUNT

Arrange a treasure hunt where groups are given Church-related clues (large and spacious building could be a mall, Tower of Babel could be a tall building), and end up at someone's home for refreshments served on "golden" paper plates.

—Trent Thomas, Kansas City, Kansas

Variations: *Give instructions using scripture references (take as many steps as the scriptures say the ark was cubits long or count the same number of houses as the Article of Faith that talks about being subject to kings).*

WORKING TOGETHER

We learn a lot about one another when we work together to make something. As a group, make ice cream, doughnuts, cookies, cake, pizza or pull taffy together. Everyone can bring different ingredients.

—Mary Lois Gunnell, Orem Utah

Variations: *Stay and eat together or take your creations to a family in need. Have everyone put one arm behind them and work together cracking eggs or sifting flour, make some of the group wear blindfolds and pair them with people who can see but can't use their hands. Make dinner together assigning everyone a different job. There can be competitions on flapjack flipping or pizza dough tossing to stimulate interest and fun. Make sure people are assigned to stay and clean up after everyone eats. Package leftovers for the missionaries.*

KITE FLYING

Have everyone meet in a place where there are wide open spaces with no trees or electrical wires. Everyone or every family or group must bring a kite. They can be purchased or homemade. Awards can be given for the longest tail, the most colorful kite, or the highest flyer.

Variations: *Hold other contests for frisbee throwing, paper airplane flying, or races for boats made from sticks.*

VISIT THE PUBLIC LIBRARY

Pick a topic of interest to the group, to pairs, or to individuals. Study that topic and report to each other. Topics could be pre-assigned or for a faster actvivty, prepare a treasure hunt with the clues hidden between pages of books that must be looked up.

PANELS

Invite a group of adults and/or peers to serve as the panel and have them respond to questions about issues of interest to your participants. Have anonymous questions submitted in advance if necessary. Questions and answers could deal with dating, manners, child rearing, keeping a courtship going after marriage, dress and grooming, etc.

Variations: *In smaller groups, have different people assigned to sit on the panel or be the Emcee. Have people take on the names of past Church leaders or scripture characters and answer modern day questions the way they would have in their day. Play a match game where all the panelists write their responses. Participants get points when their answers match.*

POSITIVE PICKET SIGNS

Pick a member of your ward or neighborhood who could use a boost, or who needs to know he or she is appreciated. Make "positive" picket signs and picket in front of the house while singing "Jolly Good Fellow." Signs could say things like "Up with Sister Jones" or "We love our Bishop!"

Variations: *Hang banners on the houses, painted rocks stacked on the driveway, or post for-sale type signs in the yard with positive messages.*

HEART ATTACK

"Attack" someone you love with hearts. Cut out paper hearts and write loving messages. Secretly tape the hearts to the window of your victim's car or his/her front door. Leave a sign that says, "You've been 'Heart Attacked.'" It's a positive way to say you like someone without leaving a huge mess to clean up.

—*Jerry Hinckley, Fremont, California*

Variations: *Give someone a "ticket" by placing a traffic ticket-sized paper in his/her car window that has positive things written on it.*

QUORUM OR CLASS EXCHANGE

Invite a quorum or class within your stake to join you in an activity. Obtain clearance from your bishop to invite the other group. Send invitations to a well-planned activity. After, send a note thanking them for coming.

—*The Activity Book*, LDS, 1977, p.150

Variations: *Make the exchange an overnighter with a group that is further away. Arrange the exchange with a foreign speaking branch or ward in your area.*

SOUND SCAVENGER HUNT

Groups are sent out with tape recorders and given a list of sounds they must record. (Toilet flushing, clock ringing, cash register ringing, etc.) They are given a time limit. When they report back, tapes are played and fun experiences shared.

—*Trent Thomas, Kansas City, Kansas*

Variations: *Use video cameras, make the items Church related (someone singing a primary song or saying an Article of Faith.)*

PAPER MACHE SCULPTURE

Old newspaper and paste are inexpensive and large numbers of people can be involved at the same time creating sculptures out of paper mache.' You can do larger items by creating a frame of paper sacks, sticks, and chicken wire. Get ideas rolling by working around a theme, having a contest, or centering on a scripture story or character. For a challenge, try recreating the monument to women or other famous sculptures. Things can get messy, so make sure good clothes are covered along with floors and table tops. Finished products can be displayed and/or given to small children.

Variations: *Try snow sculpture, mud sculpture, or sand sculpture. Poster paint mixed in can add colors. Try staying with a Church theme like temples, covered wagons, or the best tower of babel ever created (well, second best).*

BARGAIN SHOPPING CONTEST

Where's the best buy in town on a list of different items? Give each group $3 or $4 and see who can purchase the most exciting meal.

Variations: *With small groups only and having obtained permission, have half of the group gather a certain number of items from the shelves of a store. They then give the carts to the second half of the group and have to replace every item as quickly as they can. Try library books or some sort of treasure hunt where the items in the store, once found, complete a puzzle (Ye are the SALT of the earth or the dove returned with an OLIVE leaf).*

DON'T OVERLOOK THE SIMPLE THINGS

Often, simple ideas are also inexpensive. When planning an activity, don't overlook the simple things that are inherently fun and that bring the kind of joy that will strengthen relationships. Following is a list of simple activities that can be fun by themselves or enhanced by your creativity:

Go on a bike ride
Wash all the dogs in the neighborhood
Swing at the park
Build a dam in a stream and wade
Have a sunrise hike and breakfast
Have a hayride and sing-a-long
Climb trees
Go on a sight-seeing tour of your city
Have a coloring contest
Hold a bubble blowing contest
Put together model cars
Read children's books to children or just to each otherHave a waffle dinner
Have a cake walk
Go window shopping
Walks in the rain/playing in puddles
Go tubing or ice skating
Take advantage of Church Educational System programs like "Know Your Religion," or "Education Days" if available.
Temple visits

MAKE YOUR OWN MINIATURE GOLF COURSE

Using simple throw away items such as boxes, paper towel tubes, and cans, create your own miniature golf course. Invite younger people to come and try it out. Do it with a time limit and have different classes or groups responsible for one hole each. Award prizes for the most creative or detailed hole.

Variations: *Don't use clubs. Rather, hit golf balls with brooms or with your feet. Also, try a miniature bowling alley, or croquet game.*

SPORTS WITH SOMETHING MORE

Sports, in and of themselves, are not always fun group activities. Those who do well at them enjoy the activity while those who don't do well, don't have fun. Also, most groups at a given activity are too large to play most sports as they should be played. So, play them as they shouldn't be played. Add something that will put the skilled and unskilled, practiced and unpracticed on equal ground. For example, blind-folded miniature golf, three-legged pairs playing soccer or basketball, one-armed volleyball, or hockey played with brooms. Even observers have more fun watching a game when something different has been added.

—Robin Gunnell, Debbie Hawkins, Orem, Utah

Variations: *Rather than "outs" determining which team is up, work with time limits, or go through the entire batting order. When running several different games, set up game "stations" and have players rotate through the stations each time a signal is given.*

BIKE RODEO

Set up different obstacles in the Church parking lot (folding chairs and tables, cardboard boxes, etc.) that people have to ride through on bikes. Do some relays too. These can be as fun to watch as they are to participate in.

—Sean Tuttle, Salt Lake City, Utah

Variations: *Have a rodeo with tricycles, big wheels, wagons pulled by a team, roller skates, skate boards, homemade carts or "junkmobiles."*

IF THE SHOE FITS

Have the young ladies bring an old shoe (an army boot or out-of-style slipper) and have the young men pick out a shoe without knowing who it belongs to. Pair up the boys with the girls who brought the shoes for a practice date, dinner or activity. The theme could be centered around Cinderella.

—Denise Wilde, Salem, Oregon

Variations: *Instead of shoes, use hair ribbons, scarfs, or baked goodies. Try the same idea without a line-up date or, have all the group members put a shoe in and sort the shoes by color, lace type or some other criteria. The corresponding groups must then sit together or be responsible for different aspects of an activity or service project.*

★ PLANTERS WITH YOUR COLORS

Obtain permission to be responsible for one of the flower beds at the Church. Have the young women plant flowers and plants that are the colors of their Young Women values. As they see and care for the planter, it will be a constant symbolic reminder of their values and goals.

—Cinda Rollins, American Fork, Utah

Variations: *The primary could plant with primary colors. Boy scouts could plant patriotic colors. Paint things with your colors—eggs, mail boxes, toys, ceramics, wooden shapes.*

★ THUMBPRINT CARDS

Even the smallest children can be included in this activity. After placing several of your own prints on a folded paper, use your creativity and make a piece of art. Thumb prints can turn into fish or birds or eyes and teeth of a larger animal. Two together can be a bicycle. However they turn out, they become a personalized and inexpensive greeting card from your group.

—Michael and Maria Moody, Bountiful, Utah
Ensign, *December, 1980, p.46*

Variations: *Dip a string in paint, fold a paper around it and then pull the string through. Scribble on a paper and then pass it to someone and have them turn it into a picture. Melt crayons onto a paper using many colors and then create a picture from the drippings. Cards can be sent as thank-you's or holiday greetings or letters to missionaries.*

MINI MISSIONS

Send out mission calls to your group and tell them to report to a certain place that has been designated as the MTC. There, teach them about the importance of missionary work and some basic missionary skills (teaching the steps of prayer or how to introduce the Book of Mormon to a friend). Then, actually take your participants tracting. Foreign dinners could be provided in pre-assigned mission homes, where the father can act as the mission president. Staging a small homecoming will give the participants all a chance to report on their feelings and experiences and share their testimonies.

—*Scott and Angel Anderson, Bluffdale, Utah*

Variations: *Write letters to the full time missionaries from your area. Invite full time missionaries to share testimonies. Make name tags and memorize scriptures. Set up a family to play the role of friendly investigators. Participants answer questions or teach a discussion they have prepared.*

MISSIONARY SURVIVAL SEMINAR

Open with a hymn, prayer and short talk to set the proper tone. Have instructors teach participants how to sort and wash clothes, sew buttons, iron a shirt, press a suit, remove spots, prepare simple meals, wash dishes, etc. The more activities that can actually be hands-on, the better.

—*The Activity Book*, LDS, 1977, pp.7-8

Variations: *Turn it into an olympics. Teams must complete missionary-related tasks and are given points for how well they do and how fast they go. Groups can sew on buttons, iron a shirt, memorize a scripture, follow a recipe, ride a bike through an obstacle course. Try having participants work together in zones or districts.*

—*Chris Wilcox, Provo, Utah; Dean Nelson, Orem Utah*

MISSIONARY WEEKEND

Organize group into sets of companions and arrange to have each pair spend the night at the house of one or the other. Have them arise at 6:30, fix their own breakfast, have companionship study and participate in other mission-related activities throughout the day.

—*The Activity Book*, LDS, 1977, p.7

MISSIONARY WORLDS FAIR

Ask returned missionaries to provide tables with souvenirs of the countries or states in which they served. This could include some examples of food and costume and customs of other parts of the world. Participants can roam freely from station to station or rotate. Younger participants could be challenged by having them learn how to say the name of the Church in at least four languages throughout the evening.

CELEBRATE BIRTHDAYS FROM THE PAST

To interest your group in family history or simply to honor great people of the past, celebrate the birthdays of people out of their own books of remembrance. You could also look up birthdays of past presidents of the Church or famous characters in history. Plan a typical birthday party complete with balloons, cake, and ice cream. Rather than gifts, have everyone bring and share some information about the life of the person being honored or better yet, write down personal goals that they will work on to be more like great people of the past.

—*Deanna J. Hoyt, Laramie, Wyoming,* Ensign, *April, 1978, p.61*

Variations: *Visit graves of the honored person, do cake decorating using principles or events from the person's life, play party games tailored to that person, etc.*

FROM THE ATTIC

Mothers, fathers, or leaders are invited to bring something of great sentimental worth. They are given time to explain why it is important to them and why they have chosen to give it to their sons, daughters or others. Then they present that treasure to the person.

—*Vivian Cline, Draper, Utah*

Variations: *Give gifts of self—something homemade, service, poems or thoughts that have personal meaning.*

LETTERS TO POSTERITY

Have participants write letters to their future posterity after discussing what their ancestors might have written to them. Encourage participants to save some special things that will someday have meaning to their posterity.

—McArthur Family, Edmond, Oklahoma

Variations: *Have participants write letters to themselves to be delivered several years in the future. Gather the letters and put them in a place where you will remember to send them a few years down the road. Have them record goals, names they might give their your children, or what they are looking for in a mate.*

A THIRTIES DINNER

Advertise the dinner as a Thirties dinner. When guests arrive, take them through a soup line (Breads and soups) like in the depression.

—Carole Crockett, Phoenix, Arizona

Variations: *Dinners based on another decade, or focus on holidays, special historical events such as the end of World War II, the moon landing or Church history events such as Pioneer day or the restoration of the Priesthood. Photocopy library materials from the chosen time period and spread these copies out as place mats or table coverings. This makes for a fun activity, inexpensive table coverings, and easy clean up.*

—Rosanne and Britt Ripley, Mesa, Arizona

TIME CAPSULE PREDICTIONS

Usually, a time capsule is a fun way to preserve the present and enjoy the past. However, by putting in predictions for the near future, you can have a fun activity without having to wait so long before you open the capsule. For example, have everyone in the group write down predictions for the next few years. What will happen to different members of the Church, where people will be called on their missions, what changes there will be in Church leadership, who will have more children and what they will be, what callings in the ward will they be serving in, etc. Save the information and mark on your calendar to gather the same group in the future and enjoy the laughs. Making a video or a cassette of the experience might be more entertaining.

—Robin Gunnell, Orem Utah

ROCK AND ROLL

Gather a group of smooth, fist-size rocks and paint messages or symbols of love and friendship on them. Without getting caught, deliver the rocks in a pile on someone's doorstep.

> **Variations:** *Ring the doorbell and run or spell out a word on the driveway or lawn using the rocks.*

IT'S IN THE BAG

At the beginning of the activity, distribute brown paper bags. All participants go from room to room where they play short games, have mini-lessons, or question and answer periods. In each place they earn squares of white toilet paper to put inside their bags. At the end of the evening, each person examines the contents of his or her bag. The analogy is drawn that the bags represent each of us, and that we are completely in control of what goes inside of us, and what we make of ourselves.

—Libby Dutrow, Fremont, California

> **Variations:** *Use different colors of toilet paper to represent good choices or bad choices. Incorporate into the activity the idea of service by sharing squares with each other.*

ADAPTABLE FROM YOUTH TO SINGLES

PRE-CONFERENCE PEN PALS

As part of advertising for the conference, assign each one of the participants the name of another participant from another ward or stake. They must write a letter, describing themselves and what they are looking forward to at the conference. This can be done during regular Church meetings if there is concern about poor follow-through. Not only does this advertise the conference, it gives everyone something to look forward to at the beginning of the conference.

—Kris Plummer, Janet Coleman, Servicemens' District, Japan

Variations: *Have them exchange the letters without revealing their names; then they have the fun of trying to find each other at the conference.*

STAKE SHARING

Rather than going to a university campus for youth conference, make arrangements with a stake in another city and have them host you. Everyone stays in host homes and, though the activities are all done at the stake center, it is a new place for you and new folks to mingle with.

—Jack Marshall, Glendora, California

Variations: *The following year, or half-year,*

your stake can host them for a similarly rewarding experience.

PAGEANT OR PROGRAM

Rather than a traditional conference, involve everyone by preparing a program or presentation. Decide how extensive the rehearsals should be based on your choice of program—from a song with a slide show to an all-out pageant. Programs can be a time of real pulling together and bonding. It can be a real learning experience. Nothing seems to get a message in your head better than when you have to teach or present it to others.

—Marie Smith, Hacienda Heights, California

Variations: *Various LDS program scripts are available at reasonable cost or create your own. Try performing the program in several different chapels or as a service project in a hospital or rest home.*

FAMILY GROUPS

At a conference, divide participants into family groups of about ten. This will allow for mixing among the wards and peer groups. Group leaders can be assigned and families can wear distinguishing colors.

—Marie Smith, Hacienda Heights, California

Variations: *Divide conference participants into groups—"twig" groups (almost a branch). These groups will be helpful in organizing workshops, service projects, eating, etc. They can be the unit used for roll call, giving out information and announcements, morning and evening prayers, etc.*

—Courtney Lassiter, Gilbert, Arizona

THEMES FROM GOALS

Conference themes should be developed from your goals, rather than your goals coming from your theme. For example, if your committee decided that the youth need to learn to be good examples, then themes such as "Let Your Light Shine" or "The World is Watching" would be appropriate. Take the time to determine what specific goals you want to accomplish at the conference, then develop a theme to complement those goals. Sample Themes:

Let Your Light Shine
The World is Watching
Lovin' Life
You're Not Alone
That's You . . . That's Me Pullin' Together
The Big Picture—Where Do I Fit In?
The Best is Yet to Come
Shall the Youth of Zion Falter? No!
Celestial Gold—Torch Bearers of Light
A Royal Generation
It's Kind to Be Kind to the Kind and all Other Kinds Too!
Heaven . . . Don't Miss it for the World!
Take a Stand: Make a Difference
Be the Best You
The Light Within
Come Unto Christ
The Dawn of Perfection
Now and Forever
The Whole Armor of God
Reaching for the Gold
The Rising Generation
All That Glitters is not Gold
Choose You This Day
Keeping the Lord in Sight
Discovering New Horizons
I'll Help You Home
Earth and Beyond
Truth and Consequences
Walk With Me

Variations: *Themes can also be acronyms. For example S.T.O.M.P., means "Students Trying Out Moroni's Promise" or MTC—"Making The Choice or Making Things Count."*

—Barbara Miller, Orem, Utah
Brian Christensen, Lynnwood, Washington.

★ THEME SONG

Select a hymn or song that goes along with your theme (or select a theme from the lyrics of a song). Sing the song at the start of every activity of the conference: in workshops, devotionals, testimony meeting, etc. By the end of the conference everyone will know the song well. More importantly, when they sing or hear the song again it will bring back spiritual memories of the conference.

Variations: *Develop a conference cheer or chant or even a honk for your car horns.*

A CULMINATING EVENT

Let the conference be the culminating event of several months or a year's theme or focus. For example, if your focus is on reading the Book of Mormon, January is the kick-off. In February go to a close LDS visitor's center or view a video on the Book of Mormon. In March, pass out ribbons that must be worn on the same day as a reminder to read. April might be time to share copies of the Book of Mormon with friends and then report. In May, schedule a marathon reading day when everyone can catch up on their assignments. Activities continue until the conference which ties everything together.

—*Barbara Miller,* Latter-Day Woman, *Winter, 1989-90, pp.24-25*

Variations: *At the conference, video clips of each activity can refresh memories. Try presenting awards to different individuals or groups who really went the extra mile.*

A ONE-DAY YOUTH CONFERENCE

A one-day youth conference can eliminate housing costs, and minimize food expense.

A Sample One-day Agenda

9:00	am	Opening Exercises
9:15	am	Keynote Address
10:00	am	Workshop I
11:00	am	Workshop II
12:00	noon	Lunch
1:00	pm	Service Project or Mingle Games or Activity
3:00	pm	Changing clothes time
3:15	pm	Testimony Keynote Address and meeting
5:30	pm	Cleanup and goodbyes

— OR —

5:30	pm	Dinner
6:30	pm	Dance preparation
7:00	pm	Dance
9:30	pm	Closing remarks (Stake President or Bishop)
9:45	pm	Cleanup and goodbyes

If the conference is going to be a two-day affair, have the keynote address and dance the evening before. See the DANCES section for more information about putting on a dance.

USE CHURCH-OWNED FACILITIES

Hold the conference at the Stake Center rather than a college campus or resort to reduce facility costs.

Variations: *Utilize Church-owned camps, farms, or land that might be close by for activities, games, or a site for a dinner that might be new or out of the ordinary.*

HOST HOMES

Having the youth stay at "host homes" in the local area for more than one-day conferences gives the feeling of still being away. Host families can be asked to provide some meals as well.

Variations: *Have males stay over-night at the chapel while the females stay in host homes. Passwords or names for the different homes can add a new feeling. Try homemade gifts, tokens or name cards.*

MAKE YOUR OWN KIND OF MUSIC

Have conference participants put on the dance using music and components from their own collections rather than hiring a band or D.J. This can be overseen by a responsible leader.

Variations: *Have everyone bring their favorite tape and then select songs from each in turn. Arrange to use a volunteer's stereo equipment or simply use a "blaster" type tape player and place a microphone close enough that it projects over the Church sound system. On familiar songs, turn down the volume during the chorus and let everyone fill in the word until the volume is turned up again.*

COMBINE OR SKIP MEALS

Begin the conference after meal times and end just before meal times to reduce food costs. Say,

"Nothing is too good for this group and that's what we are serving—nothing. Eat before you come." Try combining some meals—have a brunch or an afternoon lupper (or would it be a sunch?).

Variations: *If there is to be a testimony meeting, perhaps an evening or morning meal can be skipped while participants are encouraged to fast.*

SACK LUNCHES

Have conference participants bring meals from home in the form of sack lunches, breakfasts or dinners.

Variations: *Contests for decorated sacks or wildest lunch boxes can add to the variety. Rather than meals, everyone can simply be asked to B.Y.O.J. (Bring your own junk food) and provide their own snacks for break time. This can save the expense of having to provide ice cream bars.*

RAP SESSIONS

In the evening, break into small groups (about 10) and find a place where your group can talk. Each group is accompanied by one leader whose job is to get the ball rolling. Then, participants can talk about anything they want. Questions can be fielded by anyone in the group. If the group is reluctant to get started, prime the pump a little with some risk questions that everyone in the group must answer in turn. These will build confidence and trust within the group and hopefully help to open the lines of communication.

—The Quintons, Lynnwood, Washington

Variations: *Some effective "risk" questions might include, "What is the best thing about the Church? What is the hardest thing about the Church? What is the best part of your face? What is something you would like to change about yourself physically? Who are you closest to in your family? Why? When was your earliest spiritual experience that you remember? Why does that experience stick out in your memory? What was it?"*

PRESENT THE RULES IN A CREATIVE WAY

Prepare a video which presents the rules in a creative way—like doing a take off on a T.V. talk show, game show or commercial.

—Lorene and Layne Kamalu, St Louis, Missouri

Variations: *Have someone dressed as Moses come in and present the rules worded as commandments. Or, have some of the leaders or participants present the rules as a song or rap.*

—Kris and Doug Plummer, Zama, Japan

Here's one rap we came up with:

Okay, now here's the situation.
We're all here during our vacation.
It's gonna be fun and it's gonna be rad
'Cause not one of us is gonna be bad.
Now it's time to shed some light
On all the rules we love to fight.
First, we're going to start this rhyme
By saying Walkmans only during free time.
Boys and girls all have their own rooms.
You're too young to be brides and grooms.
Any boy in a girl's room
Is on the road to his own doom.
At the dance, when the music slows down,
We better not see any bear hugs around.
After curfew, you better stay with your group.
That's not the time to be shooting hoop.
You've been assigned a place to sleep,
And when you're there, we won't hear a peep.
Obey the Word of Wisdom while you're here.
No coffee, tea, coke or beer.
All Church standards will apply.
Don't cuss, cheat, steal or lie.
Face cards, pornos and the gambling game
Are Satan's way to make you lame.
If you're tempted all the same,
You'll be out of here on the next train.
You break these rules of common sense,
You'll be sent home at your own expense.
Though you think this rap is dumb,
Just be glad, 'cause now we're done!

DANCES 5

GROUP MIXER DANCES

Invite a dance specialist to teach the group several mixer dances such as the "Bunny Hop," "Buzz's Mixer," "Hitchhike Shuffle," "Hokey Pokey," "Conga Line," etc. If these are unknown, find instructions in books at the local library or, better yet, create and title your own mixer dance by putting a few easy and basic steps together and repeat them throughout the song.

Variations: *Invite a guest to discuss some of the discipline required in ballet, ballroom, or modern dance. Arrange for a floor show or demonstration. Assign different groups in your ward or stake to learn and present folk dances from around the world.*

SQUARE DANCE

Arrange for an experienced specialist to teach basic square dance steps and movements. Invite a caller or use square dance records (usually available at your local library or school district). Dress as pioneers and establish a western theme and setting. Have the dance in a barn if possible.

—*The Activity Book*, LDS, 1977, p.82

Variations: *Teach the square and allow the groups to modify the basic moves in keeping with a theme or team name. For example, a team named "Keep it Clean" might promenade and doe-see-doe with dust pans and brooms in hand. Give a prize for creativity.*

DRESS UP

Changing what people wear is a good way to add variety and spice to the dance. For instance, make it a black and white evening, a fifties dance, a pajama party, a D.I. dance (wearing old clothes) etc. If participants are reluctant to go all out on dressing up, try focusing on things they can put over their regular clothes without much effort. Try crepe paper ties or headbands, hats, sunglasses, T-shirts, belts or gloves.

Variations: *Hold a "Famous Couple Dance" (Excellent for Student or Singles Wards). Assign couples in the ward to dress up as famous couples, and come to the dance in costume. Assignments can range from Fred and Wilma Flinstone to Ronald and Nancy Reagan. Give awards for the best costumed couples.*

DISC JOCKEY OR LIVE BAND?

If you decide to have the music done for you, here are a few things to keep in mind:

LIVE BANDS:

Advantages: A visual "show," local talent, etc.

Disadvantages: Usually take breaks, limited repretiore, usually more expensive than DJ's, more equipment set-up required.

DISC JOCKEYS:

Advantages: Versatile, music can be stopped and started to play games etc., able to play requests, no breaks needed, cheaper than bands, short set-up time.

Disadvantages: Not as fun to watch.

DANCE TO THE BEAT OF YOUR OWN DRUMMER

Have everyone bring a Walkman and dance to the music in their headphones—guaranteed not to disturb the neighbors!

Variations: *Have everyone bring their blasters or boom-boxes, place them around the edge of the room and tune them to the same radio station. Or park your cars in a circle and tune all the car radios to the same station.*

DANCE CARDS

Give everyone who enters the dance a card to be signed by all the partners that person dances with. Have a contest to see who can dance with the most people.

> **Variations:** *To insure that the cards are really being used, have refreshments available to only those who can show a certain number of different signatures. Have a short piece of music such as the Jeopardy theme song and play it after each dance allowing time to have everyone sign each others cards without an awkward silence. The repeated music will also serve as a reminder.*

WHO AM I? DANCE

Assign everyone an alias (according to gender) by putting a "Hello I'm . . ." sticker on his or her back. Don't allow the person to know who they're supposed to be. They must mingle and are allowed to ask only "Yes" or "No" questions to ascertain their identity.

> **Variations:** *Later, after everyone knows who they are, you can further facilitate mingling by placing travel posters around the room and making periodic announcements like, "Will Donald Duck please meet Martha Washington in Greece."*

CINDERELLA DANCE

Have all the young women take off their shoes and place them in the middle of the gym floor. The young men each grab a shoe (or two) and find the girl to whom it belongs. When he finds the mate he gets to dance with her. This is effective in getting everyone dancing.

> **Variations:** *Have the young women bring a character shoe (an army boot or out-of-fashion shoe from a Thrift store) that the boys can pick from. This way if one gets misplaced or lost no one will be too upset.*
>
> *—Shauna Curtis, Corpus Cristi, Texas*

SNOWBALL DANCE

Pick a couple to start dancing at the first

dance. Have the DJ stop the music every few moments, and wait for the boy and girl to find new partners. This continues until all are dancing.

Variations: *With smaller groups, have all the boys on the inside of a large circle and the girls on the outside. Each time the music stops, the inside circle rotates and all receive a new partner.*

SELECT GROUP DANCE IDEAS

Have the DJ announce that the dance as "girl's choice," or only for those wearing blue or green, etc.

Variations: *Try having a short dance just for chaperons or Church leaders. Rather than playing the entire song, pause the music every so often during one song and say, "Now, we need everyone who has a relative on a mission." On the next pause say, "Add to them now all those who have more than seven in their family." With each pause, the requirements should be more and more general to include everyone by the end of the song.*

PUBLICITY

Focus on getting a good turnout for the dance. With numbers come the excitement and positive attitudes that make for successful social experiences. To cut publicity costs, try mini-flyers. Rather than using a whole sheet, put two or four copies on one sheet and cut the papers. Start a calling campaign where several make calls to people who then are asked to make calls to others.

Variations: *Try door to door verbal invitations or mini posters (cutting a poster board in two).*

VIDEO PROJECTION DANCE

Obtain necessary authorization, and invite units to prepare a short video clip featuring the members of their unit. Preview the tapes and project them on the wall or a large screen during the dance.

—Dennis M. Richardson, Central Point, Oregon

Variations: *This idea could also be expanded and units could be requested to make their own music video of an approved song to play at the dance.*

★ GENERAL GUIDELINES

Here are some general guidelines reprinted from the *Ensign* (September 1987, pp. 49-50) regarding church dances.

President Ezra Taft Benson has counseled young men and young women to "take full advantage of the Church programs," encouraging them to "attend dances where the music and the lighting and the dance movements are conducive to the Spirit." Both those who plan and those who attend dances are often confused about the Church's guidelines and standards for dances. A *Priesthood Bulletin*, dated June 1982, suggests the following general guidelines:

"In providing opportunities for youth and others to help plan and carry out dance activities, priesthood leaders should counsel with those involved to pay strict attention to—

a. **Lyrics.** The lyrics should contain nothing contrary to gospel principles.
b. **Beat.** The beat, whether instrumental or vocal, should not overshadow the melody.
c. **Lights.** Lighting should be bright enough to see across the room. Psychedelic lighting designed to pulsate with the beat of the music is not acceptable.
d. **Sound.** The volume of the music should be low enough to allow two persons standing side by side to carry on a conversation without shouting."

For additional guidance, some of the most-asked questions are listed below, along with their answers:

Does the Church have a list of approved music for dances?

No. Keeping a list current would be impossible. For youth dances, it is advisable to form a youth committee whose members work with adult leaders to ensure that all lyrics and music are in harmony with church guidelines.

How can we be sure that the band we hire adheres to Church standards—both in music and conduct?

A Performance Contract (PXMU0028), available at no charge from local church distribution centers, can be used when hiring a live orchestra or band. The contract will help insure that the performers maintain appropriate conduct and standards while playing for the dance.

What about chaperons?

If the dance is for young people, chaperons are needed. Adult leaders should be invited on a rotating basis to fill this assignment. They should also be responsible for the hall, music, refreshments, and floor-show entertainment.

Are dances only for Church members?

No. In many communities, Church dances may be one of the only forms of wholesome recreation. Non-members should be welcomed, as long as they uphold Church standards while at the dance.

How can we maintain our established dress standards?

Before the dance, adult leaders should review with the youth the dress guidelines established by the local priesthood leaders. Some wards and stakes publicize the dances with posters around the community, with a statement about standards for dress and conduct on the posters so that those who attend will know what to expect. Be firm, but avoid turning anyone away for minor dress standards violations. (Non-members may not know about the standards and may not have the time or the means to go home and change.) Be courteous to everyone, especially to those you cannot admit.

How do we stop young people from "bear-hugging," or hanging on each other, at dances?

Most youth who dance "bear-hug" style do so because they don't know other dances. Give them attractive alternatives such as mixers or dance instruction in small segments throughout the evening. Capitalize on the popularity of country music by teaching the round, square, or folk dances. A youth committee, working with adult leaders, can also make up a dance card that specifies that "bear-hugging" is not permitted.

Is break-dancing permissible at Church dances?

Break-dancing and other fad dances should be considered "show" dances—not social dances—and should be treated as such. Perhaps a floor show of break-dancing could be a feature of the evening.

LOOK FOR POSITIVE

Rather than focusing on those dancing inappropriately or not participating, reward those who are involved and who are doing it right. Pass out cards redeemable for refreshments, a chance to request a favorite song, or a mini candy bar. This makes the chaperons friends rahter than enemies and creates a more positive climate at the dance.

—Ned & Judy Lunt, San Antonio, Texas

APPLE BAR

Have everyone bring an apple or an orange and provide toppings and dips. Try also a potato bar and provide sour cream, butter, gravy, grated cheese, etc.

Variations: *Extend the bar idea to bread. Have different people bring their favorite spreads for breads—jams, jellies, peanut butter, etc. Slice some loaves of hot, homemade bread and let everyone garnish their slice as they wish.*

—Val C. Wilcox, Provo, Utah

DECORATE-AS-YOU-GO BAR

Set up a buffet table with decorations for cupcakes. The first stop is frosting and after that, participants select what candies or sprinkles they will place on top of their treat as they walk down the table. Judges can be placed at the end of the table and give prizes to the most creative. Costs can be cut by asking everyone to bring a bag of favorite small candies to the activity or fireside.

—Robin Gunnell, Debbie Hawkins, Orem, Utah

Variations: *Try cookies using seasonal themes or graham crackers, snack crackers with cheeses or Rice Crispy squares.*

GIANT BANANA SPLIT

Make a huge tray out of foil that is the length

of your table or counter top. Everyone pitches in by slicing bananas, pouring syrups, squirting whipped cream and sprinkling nuts. Then, give everyone a spoon—and the more squeamish a bowl—and have at it. Cost can be cut by having everyone assigned to bring a different item.

—Robin Gunnell, Debbie Hawkins, Orem, Utah

Variations: *Try a giant burrito by overlapping flour tortillas the length of the table. Put on the toppings and fold the tortillas closed.*

—Lynncabbage Family, Fremont, California

REFRESHMENT BOBBING

Everyone has heard of apple bobbing during the Fall. Expand the idea and do some refreshment bobbing at the end of your activity. Try doughnuts that are tied with string and hung from the ceiling. Participants have to eat without the use of their hands. Or, have them eat a piece of pie or jello without using their hands.

Variations: *If you have a large group to feed, serve most of them normally while a few good-sports volunteer to bob for their portion as everyone else watches.*

WEDDING CAKE

After a family wedding, volunteer your left-over cake for the next function. Or, approach a family after a wedding for permission to freeze lower layers of the wedding cake (that usually get thrown out or forgotten). Use it as a refreshment for a ward dinner or fireside. Members can bring ice cream to serve with the cake and help to moisten it after freezing.

—Venita Law, Provo, Utah

Variations: *Contact people in the ward who are having open houses for various reasons and gather left-over baked goods for up coming events or to make packages for missionaries.*

CANDY BAR MESSAGES

Have participants bring candy bars and using the names of the candy, create a motivational message having to do with the theme of the evening or conference with the candy they have. (We'll have MOUNDS of fun while we SNICKER at the BIG HUNKS). Once messages are shared, all can enjoy the refreshment.

Variations: *Surprise everyone who brought the candy by using it to make thank you cards or appreciation posters for missionaries or people in the ward. Then, provide another type of refreshment.*

★ CANDY BAR MIX AND MATCH

Everyone is invited to bring their favorite candy bar to the activity. They are gathered, cut into bite-size pieces and put out on serving plates. During refreshments, everyone may select four or five tastes of different candy bars on napkins.

Variations: *Make candy bar shakes. Milk and ice cream are already provided. Everyone has to bring his own favorite candy bar. At the end of the evening, each person's crushed candy bar is blended with a little milk and several scoops of ice cream.*

—Carole Crockett, Phoenix, Arizona

★ AFTER-THE-SEASON CANDY

After holidays, when candy goes on sale, purchase enough for your next gathering. Freeze your bargains and save until the same holiday on the following year or melt and remold the candy into whatever you wish.

—Ann Cobb & the Stake Young Women Presidency, Little Rock, Arkansas

Variations: *Hold a Christmas party in July and eat the candy out of your stockings or a Halloween party in April and eat the Trick or Treat goodies.*

★ EAT THE CENTERPIECES OR DECORATIONS

Assign different members of the group (or groups in the ward or stake) to bring an edible centerpiece (gingerbread house, candy tree, Rock candy mountain, etc.). Along with providing the decorations throughout your fireside or program, they provide the refreshment.

Variations: *Have a Gingerbread house making contest! This way you can make the centerpieces and eat them at the end of the party.*

Divide into small groups, give each group a supply of graham crackers, small candies, and frosting for mortar. Be sure to take pictures of the finished projects.

—Soderberg Family, Salt Lake City, Utah

CHOCOLATE HEAVEN

Serve only items made of chocolate (and other extras for those who can't eat chocolate). Try assigning chocolate chip cookies, brownies, fudge, chocolate mousse and ice cream, chocolate covered nuts, raisers, and pretzels, etc.

—Ann Cobb & the Stake Young Women Presidency, Little Rock, Arkansas

Variations: *Have a chocolate dipping party with the candy fondant centers pre made. Then, everyone can make his choice, dip his own chocolate, and lick his own fingers.*

—Val C. Wilcox, Provo, Utah

COLD CEREAL PIG OUT

Have everyone bring a box of favorite cold cereal. The ward or Stake can provide the milk, paper bowls, and spoons. People can mix and match and the variety of having cold cereal in the evening is always fun.

Variations: *Watch videos of Bugs Bunny or other Saturday morning cartoons. Try inviting everyone to wear their house robe and slippers.*

DREAM DESSERT

Have participants go through magazines and cut out pictures of their dream dinners or desserts. The "meal" should be parts of several pictures cut out and pasted together and not just one delicious looking picture. The creation must be original. When everyone is done dreaming, bring out the cookies or brownies to end the evening.

Variations: *The cut out pictures can be used to make cards, messages or posters for ward or stake leaders, teachers or parents.*

FONDUE POT WITH NEW RULES

Gather around a fondue pot, or several pots

depending on the size of your group, and enjoy dipping marshmallows, fruit, etc. into the melted chocolate. Make it funnier by blowing a whistle and making a new eating rule with every blow. For example, one time you must feed the person to your left. Next time you must do it one at a time with your eyes closed. After that, those who drop what they're dipping must kiss the person next to them on the cheek.

—*Robin Gunnell, Debbie Hawkins, Orem, Utah*

Variations: *Try cheese fondue with veggies and crackers if you are not in the mood for something sweet.*

★ SHORTENING FOOD LINES

Set up identical serving tables spaced out across the cultural hall. Allow people to go down both sides of each table.

—*Beth Duering, Salt Lake City, Utah*

Variations: *Call families or groups to go to different lines in creative ways. For example, "All families who have a letter "p" in their last names or all people who have roots in Denmark."*

★ MUSICAL REFRESHMENTS

Everyone brings his favorite candy bar. As music is played, a few candy bars are passed around the circle. When music ends, those who have the candy bars are excused to step out and watch as a few more candy bars are placed in the circle. Soon, everyone has one and they have had fun getting it.

—*Keith and Teresa Ramsey, Idaho*

Variations: *If you don't want to have people bring their candy, try using penny candy or even checkers or buttons that can later be turned in for something that can't be passed.*

★ DON'T BUY NAPKINS

If you're continually having refreshments for the same group of people, buy or make some washcloths rather than paper napkins and then simply reuse them.

—*Karen May, Fresno, California,* Ensign, *Oct, 1978, p.50*

Variations: *Let the group decorate their washcloths and put their name on them in a creative way. Perhaps they could put a symbol of musical notes or a football representing something they do well.*

POPCORN POTPOURRI

Assign people to bring popcorn made to their favorite recipe. Some will bring plain popcorn and others will bring a little bit of everything—cheese, caramel, chocolate, onion, etc. During refreshments, bowls can be placed out and people can enjoy selecting a variety.

—Robin Gunnell, Debbie Hawkins, Orem, Utah

Variations: *Make it a "Guess-What-It-Is?" contest or best tasting contest.*

MIXED FRUIT SALAD

Watermelons are provided and scooped out to create a bowl. Everyone who comes must bring a fruit to be prepared and tossed into the salad.

—Jon and Julie Vogl, Milwaukee, Wisconsin

Variations: *Add ice cream or frozen yogurt for a dessert treat.*

SERVE REFRESHMENTS IN A UNIQUE WAY

You may have the same old pot-luck cookies, brownies and punch that you have all the time, but you can serve it in a new way. Try using things that go along with your theme. Serve out of a boat, canoe, or fish net. Have the goodies sitting in a treasure chest or on a treasure map with the edges burned.

—Jonell Brown and Ina Lee Goforth, Hendersonville, North Carolina

Variations: *Rather than setting up tables or chairs, try having the dinner or refreshments on blankets or tablecloths spread on the floor.*

VEGGIE PEOPLE

As people select prepared vegetables and fruits from serving trays, they must create a face on their paper plate. Awards can be given for the funniest, scariest, silliest, most beautiful, etc. before everyone is allowed to dig in.

—Robin Gunnell, Debbie Hawkins, Orem, Utah

Variations: *As people at tables enjoy vegetables and dips, they also work on carving totem poles from carrots or faces out of potatoes.*

—Vela A. Smith, Family Night Fun *by Paxman, 1963. p.156*

A TASTE OF OUR WARD

Patterned after an annual activity in Chicago (called "A Taste of Chicago") in which a street is closed off and local restaurants and food businesses set up booths and offer tastes of their best dishes, you set up booths and have families in the ward offer tastes of their best deserts or finger food.

—Randal and Wendy Wright, Vidor, Texas

Variations: *This activity could be combined with Family Arts and Crafts Night.*

SERVICE 7

BABY-SITTING

Volunteer to baby-sit children so adults or friends can go to the Temple, Know Your Religion, or special firesides. Make a list of supplies to use when baby-sitting. Include different items that will instruct and entertain. (Magazines, colored paper, blunt-ended scissors, paste, modeling clay, magnets, bean bags, story books, etc.) Make surprise boxes that contain items of interest. Make a questionnaire to be filled in by parents before they leave, containing such information as emergency numbers and special instructions. As a group, discuss helps for baby-sitting and parent expectations of baby-sitters.

—*The Activity Book*, LDS, 1977, pp.18-19

Variations: *Instead of going to individual homes, provide a nursery at the chapel using the regular nursery games and facilities as well as the extra things you prepare. Priesthood holders could provide the service on homemaking night when the sisters are meeting.*

BABY QUILTS

Tie baby quilts for those in your ward who are expecting. Because such quilts are small, they don't take much time to finish. Usually, they can be started, finished, and delivered in a short period of time.

—*Val C. Wilcox, Provo, Utah*

Variations: *Quilts for many occasions. Have members of the organization all prepare their* *own square on a given theme or representing themselves and combine all the squares together for a patch work of personalized messages and memories.*

—Venita Law, Provo, Utah

A CALENDAR OF SERVICE

On a calendar, record services that participants are willing to offer someone throughout an entire year. These can be specific acts or simply marked days so the recipient knows to expect something on that day. Then, throughout the year clean up the yard, call and visit, take the recipient to a dinner or movie, wash windows, etc. on those set days.

—Sharon Ballif, Ogden, Utah, Ensign, *December, 1984, p.64*

Variations: *Assign different organizations different months of the year. Or assign an organization to make several similar calendars for each person in their group. Each person would be assigned to do an act of service on designated days.*

HOW MANY GOOD DEEDS UNTIL . . .

Using a calendar with pockets, count off the days until Christmas with small acts of service. Inside the pocket is a holiday related item with different instructions: hug three people, decorate a friends locker or room, make some goodies for someone, give away a Book of Mormon, etc. This way you are not just counting down days to Christmas, but you are also making those days count!

—Annette P. Bowen, Bellevue, Washington, Ensign, *December, 1988, p.64*

Variations: *Try the same thing for any holiday like Thanksgiving or Valentines Day. What better way to prepare for General Conferences than by counting down the days with service?*

WASH CARS

Organize a ward car wash. Use an area in the ward parking lot. Be sure to keep electric cords for vacuum cleaners away from water. If your ward geography permits, wash people's cars in their own driveways.

Variations: *Offer to wash cars passing by for free. If you are in a Church parking lot, this can leave a good impression along with an appropriate pamphlet or invitation to Church.*

GLEAN FIELDS

Arrange with farmers in your area to let your group glean their fields or orchards once the regular harvest is finished. Produce that is gathered can be shared with needy families.

—Carolyn Huish, San Juan Capistrano, California

Variations: *Offer produce to shelters for the homeless or to community kitchens.*

CANNED FOOD CAR RALLY

The groups are split into teams and assigned to go door to door in a certain ward or area asking for one canned food item. The groups meet back at the Church and report on their experiences as they pack the canned goods into boxes to be distributed to needy families.

—Marc Porter and Adam Sharp, Redmond, Washington

Variations: *If location permits, work on bikes or have each group required to put food in a little red wagon.*

GATHER FOOD ALPHABETICALLY

Turn service into a game. Rather than simply collecting canned goods for the needy in the traditional way, have your group collect one can at a time—in alphabetical order. From the first house visited, they must get a can that has the letter "A" on it and so forth. This way, it is not an imposition on the families being asked to donate since they can give no more than one can per home.

Variations: *Try gathering food by the colors on the cans, or by brand names.*

MAKING THINGS FOR CHILDREN

Rhythm Instruments:

Using household items such as cans, lids, string, paper towel rolls, burned-out light bulbs, paper plates and bowls, beans, sandpaper, paper mache, etc., make creative instruments that children can shake, scrape, pound and play safely. Prepare a band and show them how to use the instruments. Then, present the masterpieces to the nursery or to a local elementary school classroom.

—*The Activity Book*, LDS, 1977, p.94

Books:

Write your own story, illustrate a scripture story, or copy the words of a children's poem giving credit to the author and illustrate it. Attach the pages to form a booklet and present it to the nursery. Laminating the pages will help the books last longer.

—*The Activity Book*, LDS, 1977, p.103

Puzzles:

Draw or glue bold and colorful pictures from children's magazines (use the *Friend)* onto card stock-type poster paper. These can then be cut into large and simple shapes for children to put back together.

—*The Activity Book*, LDS, 1977, p.103

Dolls:

Create your own rag dolls or paper dolls or simply make clothes for some of the existing dolls and stuffed animals in the nursery. If your group does not have sewing skills, use a hot glue gun for satisfactory results.

★ WORKING WITH CHILDREN

Volunteer to assist in the Primary or Relief Society nursery, or with some other group of small children. Arrange equipment and plan activities (songs and stories) before the nursery begins. Use positive directions and avoid over-using the word "don't." Praise the children for their work and cooperation. Let the children help clean up.

—*The Activity Book*, LDS, 1977, p.18

Variations: *Make up games for children. Make up some word find puzzles, word scrambles or dot-to-dots on a Church theme. Present them to younger members of the ward as positive things to be doing on Sunday after Church.*

★ STORIES ON TAPE FOR CHILDREN

Gather some tape recorders, blank tapes, and favorite children's stories. With great expression and inflection, read and record the stories. Different voices can be used when someone is speaking. The finished tapes can be donated to a hospital, preschool, the Church nursery, or simply given to small children in your ward or neighborhood.

—*Robin Gunnell, Orem, Utah*

Variations: *Write a new story, using the child's name as one of the characters.*

CLEANING MEETINGHOUSE GROUNDS

Coordinate this activity through the bishopric and meetinghouse custodian. Organize the other wards or branches who share the building with your ward or branch. Mow and edge the lawns, rake and pick up leaves, remove weeds, cultivate flower beds, sweep walks, prune and trim trees and shrubs. Arrange for necessary trucks and equipment.

—*The Activity Book,* LDS, 1977, p.49

Variations: *Clean the grounds of community churches. Coordinate this activity through the leaders of the various Churches. (See* The New Era, *May, 1989, p.20.) This idea could be expanded to local parks, schools and city buildings as well.*

—*Mark and Michele Gunnell, Fullerton, California*

CLEANING THE MEETINGHOUSE

Arrange with the bishopric to clean the meetinghouse and have the custodian or other specialist discuss and demonstrate proper methods of cleaning. Use a checklist in making assignments and checking on work done. (Clean cupboards, ovens, refrigerator, sinks, mirrors, toilets, floors, benches, chairs, tables, blackboards and erasers, etc.)

—*The Activity Book,* LDS 1977, p.50

Variations: *Clean a house. Go top-to-bottom in one home or go through several in the ward providing an over-looked service at each: For example, replacing faucet washers, florescent light starters or filters in the furnace.*

CLEANING THE ZOO

Make arrangements to volunteer for cleaning and upkeep at a zoo. It is novel enough to be fun and does provide a very needed service for the community and the animals.

—Clotel and Palmer Spencer, Honolulu, Hawaii
(The Spencer's stake was featured in The New Era *when they cleaned the local zoo.)*

Variations: *Clean a Graveyard. Arrange to clean up a grave yard, washing down and trimming around headstones. Extra fun can be added by offering prizes for the pair or group that finds the longest last name, the oldest headstone, the most recent death, etc.*

—Trent Thomas, Kansas City, Kansas.

Try cleaning up a highway. The idea of picking up trash along a highway is not new but can be spiced up by having participants wear crazy hats or bright colored aprons. You can also have small competition for the groups who collect the most or, more fun, points for finding wrappers from certain fast foods chains or empty cans of root beer. More points can be given if trash gatherers say "Yuk, Yuk, Yuk" out loud if they come across a beer can or empty package of cigarettes (and "Yum, yum, yum" if they see a wrapper of something they would have liked).

—Wendy and Randal Wright, Vidor, Texas

★ GATHER, CLEAN, AND REPAIR CLOTHING

Make arrangements with a needy orphanage or school in a foreign country. (This can be done through governmental or charitable organizations or often recently returned missionaries from foreign counties will know of special needs.) Gather used clothes throughout your Stake or by going door-to-door in the community. Prepare the clothes and ship them. Caution: Mailing costs are expensive and in many foreign areas mail is undependable. Work through an organization that is already set up to receive this type of contribution or scale down your efforts to serve needy families that returned missionaries know how to contact or needy people in your own area.

—Charlene B. Taylor, Las Vegas, Nevada

Variations: *Find families who have recently moved to your climate and help prepare them for the summer or winter by gathering appropriate clothing. Having to re-outfit an entire* *family in a different climate can be expensive even for families with solid incomes.*

SERVICE COUPON BOOKS

Create a coupon book good for services you are willing to provide and give it to a grandparent or someone in need. Perhaps different members of your group could offer one service each that they will be willing to do several times (prepare furnace for winter, wash windows, tune up cars) the whole thing could be photocopied and distributed to your entire ward.

—*Keith and Teresa Ramsey, Idaho*

Variations: *Coupons Throughout the Year. Instead of a batch of goodies, try cooking up a batch of coupons, redeemable monthly, and mail them out to missionaries and friends. Using a sewing machine without thread, you can perforate a sheet of typing paper into twelve coupons, and on each one write a promised service. This way, service lasts throughout the entire year.*

—*Barbara Jensen, Antioch, California,* Ensign, *December, 1978, p.40*

ELF NIGHT

Take flowers, vegetables, treats, or hand made gifts to some selected families. Leave them anonymously on the door step. Everyone has done this once or twice around Christmas time, but try it at another time of year and make a night out of it. Plan your strategy for each home and challenge yourselves to not get caught.

Variations: *Do it on several consecutive nights. Visit the same families and with each delivery, leave part of a card that can be put together as a puzzle with a message of love or inspiration for the family.*

SERVICE STOCK MARKET EXCHANGE

Everyone in the group comes prepared with services they are willing to provide written on separate pieces of paper (baking a cake, cleaning the yard, washing windows, sitting children, etc.). When the trading is opened, everyone mingles, trading the services they are offering for the services they want or need. Everyone calls out at the same time trying to locate a service or get rid of one.

Once someone has traded his service to someone else, that person is free to trade it again to another party. When the market closes, everyone reads off the services they received and arrangements are made for follow through on providing their services.

Variations: *Put the service papers in a bowl and have winners of different relay-type events draw the papers as prizes.*

DECORATED GIFT BOXES

Have your group gather and decorate boxes. These can be done along a holiday theme or simply made to be bright and happy. Make it into a contest to increase motivation. Once the boxes are decorated, participants are assigned to fill the box with gifts and/or food that would be appreciated by an elderly person. Next time you gather, take the decorated and filled boxes and present them as gifts to your selected families.

Variations: *Decorate and fill boxes for missionaries or teachers in the ward. Try having one organization decorate the boxes and another organization fill them.*

ASSEMBLY LINE GOODIE BOXES

Everyone brings a plate of his or her favorite goodies. Place them all out on a table and gather one or two from each plate to create variety-packed packages to deliver to missionaries or others who might be in need.

Variations: *After a holiday such as Halloween, Christmas or Valentines, have people gather extra candy or goodies they have around the house. With no extra work you can create the variety gift packs by combining leftovers while they are all still fresh.*

PERSONAL HISTORY FOR THE ELDERLY

Arrange to visit some elderly people and have participants prepared with a list of questions about their memories. (What did you do for dates? How much money did it cost for you to go to a movie or buy a car? What are the circumstances surrounding the birth of your children? Where were you during World War II?) As those being interviewed share, their answers can be recorded by taking notes or with a tape recorder. Notes and tapes can be left with the elderly person or they can be typed and formally and presented to them for their personal history. Most elderly people love to talk and visit. However, this is a twist that makes the project participants really feel like they are giving a needed service rather than simply listening to old stories.

Variations: *Create Family History Questionnaires. Rather than asking family members to write all about their life, come up with twenty questions that will allow them to unlock specific memories. Responses can be compiled and sent to the whole family.*

—Barbara Stockwell, Springfield, Oregon, Ensign, *April, 1986, p.65*

Provide a similar service for couples who have a new baby. Interview them while their memories are fresh and record details for them that they might not remember later.

RECORD BABY BLESSINGS

Discretely record or take down in short hand the blessings that new fathers give their babies in Church. Later, type the blessing neatly and present it to the family for the baby's personal record.

—Judeth Dick, Provo, Utah

Variations: *On the day of the birth of a new baby in the ward, gather current newspapers and magazines. Later, they can be presented to the new parents who have often had a lot more on their minds than saving such things as a start to their new child's personal journal. Try recording other events in the first years of children's lives for the parents. Mothers are sometimes too busy to be keeping a detailed record of their young children's lives. An excellent service would be to prepare a questionnaire with questions such as, "What are your child's new words? What cute things has he done recently? What trouble has he been in?" etc. Responses can be noted and the same questions can be asked every few months throughout the year. At the end of the year, all the questionnaires can be* *compiled—along with pictures you have taken (at Church meetings is a good time to catch everyone) and hand prints you have made—and presented to the Mother for her child's records.*

—Terrie Colleen Card, American Fork, Utah, Ensign, *February, 1986, p.71*

HONOR A LOCAL CITIZEN OR MEMBER OF THE WARD

Choose the person you plan to honor. This should be a person who has made a noteworthy contribution to the Church or community. Obtain suggestions and approval from your bishop, stake president, or other local leaders. Find out all you can about the person to be honored. Talk with his or her spouse, children, neighbors, and friends. Plan a special program to honor this person. Have someone relate his life history and emphasize his important accomplishments. Let family members participate. Make a scrapbook about the individual. Include comments from his friends, family and neighbors.

—The Activity Book, p.209

Variations: *Present the scrapbook as the award or along with the award. You may wish to keep the evening a surprise. This is a great opportunity to submit details of the evening and the reason for the person of your choice to the local newspapers.*

GROUP LETTERS

Start several letters (to elderly ward members, local Church leaders, etc.) by putting the appropriate names at the top of the sheets. Do several at once so many can be engaged in the activity. After someone writes a short note and signs it, the paper is passed to the next person. Time limits (complete with a kitchen timer) can either push participants to write more than a few words or limit the amount of time writers can spend on each letter. Letters are collected and sent.

Variations: *Taking a picture of the group that can be included in the letter is easy and makes the notes more meaningful to the recipients. Try writing missionaries who don't get much mail. Contact local or foreign mission offices* *(or ask for names and addresses from missionaries who are serving from your own ward). Get the names of Elders, Sisters, and couples who do not get a lot of support in the form of letters and packages. Focus on those particular missionaries. Send care packages, pictures of your group, positive quotes, favorite scriptures, and most of all, letters. Don't do it just once, but many times over a series of months so that your efforts are seen as sincere caring and not simply a one-time service project.*

MAKING NEWSPAPER LOGS

Collect old newspapers. Soak newspapers overnight in water, or soak them for two hours in water to which one cup of laundry detergent has been added. Roll the newspapers on cut 1" wooden rods. Roll paper until the logs are about 4 inches in diameter. Tie each log with string and stand the rolls to dry. These can be passed out to needy families or to all members of a ward or group with a reminder about the importance placed on home production and storage by the prophets.

—*The Activity Book,* LDS, 1977, p.24

Variations: *Make arrangements to show up at a members home to update and help rotate their water storage. Old water can be dumped and containers refilled with fresh water. You could also check out 72-hour kits and make suggestions or label what has been set aside with the replacement date.*

A JAR OF LOVE

Decorate a wide mouth quart jar or an empty shortening can or a box. Inside, put about thirty slips of paper on which are written specific incidents of appreciation for what that person said or did and other reasons why we love the person to whom we are giving the jar.

—*Sharla Luker, Salt Lake City, Utah,* Ensign, *February, 1988, p.68*

Variations: *Put the little slips of paper into pill capsule containers, plastic eggs or fortune cookies.*

MILES FOR EXTRA-MILE SERVICE

Choose a final destination such as Italy and

then figure out how many miles it is away from your home. Participants earn varying amounts of miles by reaching their service goals, either personally set, or set as a group. Service to a widow might be 2,000 miles and baby-sitting for free while a couple goes to the Temple could give you 5,000. When the project comes to a close, all gather for a spaghetti dinner and the place is decorated like an Italian restaurant. Those who reached their goals are given special recognition or a special dessert.

—Debi Wilcox, Georgia Rassmusen, Provo, Utah

Variations: *Select a destination that is not as far away and earn yards or feet. Finally, you can actually go to the location for a culminating event. For example, if you are close to a Temple or Visitors Center, these would be excellent goals.*

★ SPECIAL OLYMPICS

Sponsor a Special Olympics at a home for the handicapped in your area. Work with the recreational specialist at that facility. Plan wheelchair races, walking races, frisbee throws, walker races, etc. Prepare by making some preliminary visits to the home taking in some evening treats. Introduce your olympics with a special flag ceremony and the olympic theme song.

—Charlene B. Taylor, Las Vegas, Nevada
(Sister Taylor's stake was featured in The New Era *when they held a Special Olympics event.)*

Variations: *Prepare a similar experience on a smaller scale with special education classes in local schools.*

★ PRESENTING A PROGRAM

Make arrangements with a local hospital, rest home or retirement center to present a program. Keep in mind their rules. Make sure you leave a number where you can be reached and get the name of their program coordinator who will arrange the activity with you. Decide on the program (songs, skits, readings, story telling, etc.). Make sure the program is well-practiced and not too long. Remember to coordinate transportation.

—The Activity Book, LDS, 1977, p.209

Variations: *Leave time for some mingling afterward. One-on-one visiting after a program and expressions of sincere caring are often a greater service than any songs or stories. Try adopting a resident. Make arrangements with a local rest home, retirement center, or home for the handicapped. Visit the facility, introducing participants to residents they adopt. After spending some time with them on the first visit, participants are to assess specific personal needs and follow up individually or as a group.*

—Vivian Cline, Draper, Utah

SERVICE SCAVENGER HUNT

Divide into groups and give everyone a list of different acts of service they can perform, each with different point values. Use anything from washing the car to cleaning the bird cage, to raking leaves to changing the baby. Each group is assigned their own section of the neighborhood and given a time limit in which they must return. Make sure the people whose doors you knock on know right at first that you're a church youth group and that you're not asking for money. Have the person receiving the service initial your service form. This idea appeared in *The New Era.*

Variations: *Some groups have used this activity as an opportunity to place copies of the Book of Mormon.*

—Stan and Mary Crippen, Wildomar, California

AT AN ELEMENTARY SCHOOL

Find an elementary school that is in session when your group is not. (Neighboring districts have different holidays and teacher preparation days. Also, check for year-round schools in your community. Large day care centers that operate year round would also be an option.) Arrange with the principal and faculty to bring your group in on a given morning. Participants can be paired with children and help the teacher in whatever she would like (they could read to the children, help with math or spelling, write stories that they dictate, help on computers, or do an art project). Participants can take their child "buddy" out to recess and play with them and arrangements can be made for participants to eat lunch with the children.

Variations: *Follow up with letters and pictures. Have all the participants sign a book that you can donate to the school library to remember the event.*

★ SCOUT UNIFORM CHECK OUT

Outgrown scout uniforms can be donated to a central pool to be checked out by other boys.

—Rosanne and Britt Ripley, Mesa, Arizona

Variations: *The same thing can be done with scout handbooks, merit badge books, packs, sleeping bags, cooking gear, etc.*

★ GO "SERVICE OR TREATING"

Like trick or treating, go door to door, and explain to the person who answers the door that he or she has a choice of a treat that you can give them or a quick service you are willing to provide. Go until treats are gone or until a predetermined number of acts of service are accumulated. This can be done at any time of year.

Variations: *Do a similar take-off on other holiday themes—Valentines, Memorial Day, Thanksgiving or Christmas.*

★ SERVICE WITH A SMILE

Contact local Church leaders and get phone numbers of people in the area (members and non-members) whom the young people could help. Contact each and assign several of your group to take care of the specific needs in each case. The focus is on attitude. Because participants are involved in the planning as well as the doing, it can be something they care more about. Because everyone is doing different acts of service at the same time, it seems natural to meet together and report on what each group did "with a smile."

—Charlene B. Tayor, Las Vegas, Nevada

Variations: *As a part of this or any service project, memorize the golden rule scripture, Matthew 7:12. Here is one way to remember the reference: Let's live the golden rule SEVEN days a week, TWELVE months a year!*

—Maxine Bennett, Stockton, California,
Ensign, *February, 1986, p.71*

PLANTING TREES

Have a specialist explain and demonstrate how to plant trees and shrubs. Work in groups to plant trees or shrubs and then make necessary assignments for preliminary care of the plants. Coordinate the activity with proper authorities of the meetinghouse, school or park where you are doing the service.

—*The Activity Book*, LDS, 1977, pp.49-50

Variations: *Rather than giving out the traditional Mother's Day flower in Church, go door to door in the ward and actually plant a flower somewhere in the yard or in a window box of all the mothers. The project will go quickly if participants are divided into groups.*

SERVICE AROUND THE WARD

Anonymously provide a kind service or take bread or a treat to another family in the ward. Give them a note instructing them to display a designated marker (a construction paper star or circle or something on a holiday or seasonal theme) in their front window to show that they have been served. Next, that family provides a similar service or gift to another family in the ward that doesn't yet display the star. Many variations are possible but it is a good way to make sure everyone is remembered and put people in the position of serving a family they might not know very well.

—*Roger and Moana Wilcox, Orem, Utah*

Variations: *Try the same thing in your neighborhood or apartment building involving neighbors who are not members of the Church.*

SERVE ANOTHER WARD

Arrange to serve and clean up at another ward's dinner. They might do the same for you some time.

—*Jon and Julie Vogl, Milwaukee, Wisconsin*

Variations: *Give the custodian a day off. Many people usually stay after a large meeting or fireside to take down chairs. Offer instead to set up chairs. Try putting a few messages under a few of the chairs with a suggestion to look up a particular scripture or a particular hymn number.*

WINDSHIELD WASH

Go through a crowded parking lot washing windshields and leaving notes that say something like this: While you were (in the Mall) your windshield has been washed by ( ). We are doing this as a act of service because we feel better when we are helping others. Have a great day!

Variations: *Gather shopping carts and have them ready at the door of the store with a note for the employees who will come out and see their job already done. Go from parking lot to parking lot all across town.*

REUSABLE ANNOUNCEMENT OR ADVERTISING BOARD

Laminate a color poster board, and use a grease pencil to write information about upcoming events. Before laminating, draw a nice border or picture or include headings such as Extra, Extra, or Coming Up, or Important Announcement.

—Gayle Hansen, Valencia, California

Variations: *Make a Brother or Sister-of-the-Month chart, or a Sunday School lesson board, lined with quotes, thoughts, scriptures, pictures etc.*

SILK AND ARTIFICIAL FLOWERS

Make arrangements with your local cemetery to collect left-overs after memorial day. After a while, most cemeteries will discard artificial plants and flower containers. Collect some of the nice containers along with silk leaves and flowers. They can add to many occasions and activities at no cost.

—Jonell Brown and Ina Lee Goforth, Hendersonville, North Carolina

Variations: *Decorate using weeds or wild flowers (sun flowers) that are plentiful in your area.*

DECORATE A SECTION

Rather than spending the time and effort to decorate the whole gymnasium, pick just one area to decorate. Use the entrance, a theme wall, the refreshment area, or the center of the floor. You can also partition off an area that will not be used so that it won't look "undecorated."

Variations: *For small groups, use the stage area or the portable platforms so you don't have as much territory to cover. Then, the empty hall doesn't seem so distracting.*

DIVIDING DECORATION ASSIGNMENTS

Assign different classes or groups a different aspect of the decorations. As guests arrive, give them a tally sheet and invite them to walk around and judge centerpieces or walls. This will motivate the decorators beforehand and facilitate mingling during the activity.

—Beth Duering, Salt Lake City, Utah

Variations: *On more formal occasions, invite different couples in the ward to be hosts and hostesses and be in charge of setting a table for eight. They enjoy showing off their nice dishes and centerpieces and the variety from table to table makes for a beautiful decorated tone.*

—Dixie Longwell, Provo, Utah

HELIUM BALLOONS

Balloons provide color and atmosphere. They can be secured to chairs, tables, painted bricks, or the floor to create different settings. Check for sources of helium that might be less expensive than gift or novelty stores. Try welding supply outlets.

—Jonell Brown and Ina Lee Goforth, Hendersonville, North Carolina

Variations: *Balloons can be attached to paper to give them weight and left to float freely about. Perhaps you could attach scriptures of the evening's theme.*

CARDBOARD CUTOUTS

Select a symbol (like gingerbread men) and cut out several from cardboard. Each group or quorum is assigned to return it decorated (some might paint it while others might use cotton, lifesavers or peppermint candies). Awards can make it more exciting.

—Melody Holland, Kailua, Hawaii

Variations: *Poster boards, paper table clothes, aprons, boxes, bottles, or jugs filled with flowers from their own gardens.*

PARACHUTE CEILINGS

Most elementary schools have parachutes in their PE supplies that they may allow you to borrow or rent. Hang it in the cultural hall with fishing line (fishing line is strong and can't be seen). The parachute creates a drop ceiling for a dance floor, dinner or a covered area for a circus or theater in the round.

Variations: *Try different color bed sheets suspended over each table area or simply hanging at different levels as flags.*

CHILD-MADE DECORATIONS

Have the primary children color or paint on rolls of butcher paper during sharing time in primary. Label the child's area. Later, during the activity or dinner, both parents and children enjoy looking at the part of the wall they covered.

—*Birthe S. Champenois, Copenhagen, Denmark*

Variations: *Outline the body of each child and have them draw themselves and color in clothes. The life-size bodies cover a large space. Have each child make his own face out of construction paper. Faces can be grouped and "finished" by adding scarfs for Christmas carolers, costumes for halloween, or feathers and pilgrim hats for Thanksgiving.*

INEXPENSIVE COSTUME IDEAS

Colored plastic table covering that comes in rolls can be cut, and gathered with masking tape. Staple the seams. Garbage sacks, which also come in different colors can also be used as shirts or skirts. The metallic colored bags make great space suits. Spray paint cheap fabric for needed colors or textures. For example, florescent paint for under a black light is much less than fluorescent material. After stake road shows, costumes can be gathered and then altered for the following year.

—*Rosanne and Britt Ripley, Mesa, Arizona*

Variations: *Look through the costume boxes of the ward or group members. List the fun costumes that are already available and plan* *your skit or show around what has already been made in the past.*

DOODLE CONTEST

Cover tables with butcher paper and provide crayons that families can use to doodle while they are waiting to be served or get in line. Awards can be given to the best doodle artists.

—Jon and Julie Vogl, Milwaukee, Wisconsin

Variations: *Rather than the tables, cover walls or doors.*

DECORATE DOORWAYS

By hanging crepe paper, string, or Christmas lights, around and through a doorway, you can create the desired effect without having to decorate the entire hall.

—Beth Duering, Salt Lake City, Utah

GRAFFITI WALL

Cover a wall with newsprint and put markers in dixie cups either attached to the wall or nearby. Have everyone sign the wall or do some art work. It will become quite an interesting wall and a background for picture taking.

EASEL COME, EASEL GO

Use easels and pictures, paintings or photographs from the members or from the ward library according to your theme. Easels are easy to set up, they can create a nice partition in the room, and clean-up is fast and easy too.

Variations: *Drape the easels with quilts or colored cloth. A bit of masking or duct tape on the floor or table top keeps them from slipping.*

LAMP POSTS

Using carpet rolls, make some lamp posts that are just for show, or that really light up. Lamp posts are adaptable to many holidays and object lessons on light. Lamp posts can be used to create the feel of a french restaurant or better yet, they can just be used during any dinner and help to create a nice mood in an otherwise large and empty cultural hall.

—Joan Salgy, Orem, Utah

Variations: *Create smaller, waist-high posts and drape appropriately colored ribbons or crepe paper between the posts to direct your group. Posts set on top of tables can become the center point for streamers stretching outward to create a canopy.*

★ COVER THE LIGHTS

To get rid of the glare from cultural hall lights, and to create more of an atmosphere, cover the lights with colored cellophane. Get help from those who normally change the bulbs. This is an inexpensive way to change the mood of a room for a formal dinner or dance.

—Beth Duering, Salt Lake City, Utah

Variations: *Turn on only the stage lights in the cultural hall and turn them out toward the room. Hang Saran Wrap from the middle of the cultural hall ceiling and drape it under the colored stage lights. When the lights are on, it creates a special effect at little expense.*

—Becky Crockett, Phoenix, Arizona

★ GUESS WHO?

Have numbered papers around the room with different people's finger prints or hand prints. Besides being personalized decorations, the pictures can provide an activity throughout the evening as people try to determine which person created each picture. At the end of the activity, those who were finger printed stand by their own papers.

Variations: *Use lip prints, profiles, birth date, place of birth, number of traffic tickets in the last five years, dream vacation spot, favorite scriptures or scripture characters.*

★ LOW-COST LUAU

Use folded and cut newspaper for grass skirts. Eat from abalone shells. String real leaves, flowers, and packing styrofoam on thread to create leis.

—Rosanne and Britt Ripley, Mesa, Arizona

Variations: *Use newspaper and packing styrofoam to create the hats of any country or culture using paper maché.*

★ CREATE YOUR OWN CENTERPIECE

Giving raw materials to each table, have them work together to create the most appropriate centerpiece for the theme as they wait for their dinner.

Variations: *Each group could get a wall or doorway.*

★ MOBILES

Mobiles are inexpensive, fun to create and make excellent use of space. Mobiles can be created using household materials like straws, string, fishing line, sticks and cardboard. Have a contest or assign groups to create mobiles around a theme for decoration.

Variations: *Use pictures from the Church library or from used Church magazines that can be hung around the room at different levels with string and tape.*

★ BACKGROUND MUSIC

Background music is helpful in creating atmosphere. Since the music doesn't need to be loud, Renting and moving expensive equipment is not necessary. Use the existing sound system to play music while people enter, or during or after the activity. Choose music appropriate to the activity.

Variations: *Arrange for someone to play the piano or sing with a guitar. Or, put on a tape of violin music and have someone dressed as a musician stroll from table to table and fake playing a real or imagined instrument.*

★ USE NATURAL THINGS

Nature is inexpensive but always beautiful. Use dried weeds, corn stalks, branches, wood, haystacks, autumn leaves, dried bark, moss, leaves, palm fronds, pine cones and shells.

Variations: *Ask ward members for the use of artificial Christmas trees or artificial plants for natural looking decor.*

TREE BRANCHES

Arrange to cut low branches from junk trees in open space areas or fields. The branches, when stood on end in a cultural hall, appear to be trees. These can be decorated with borrowed christmas lights, paper cut-outs, paper chains, etc., to create any desired mood.

PAPER SYMBOLS

Repeat the same symbol around the room in different sizes and colors to create atmosphere using colored paper. (Colored butcher paper purchased by the yard from craft stores.) For example, for a tropical theme, cut out brown coconut tree stumps and green leaves and branches. Repeat this pattern around the room. The only expense is paper and tape.

Variations: *As you cut out your symbol, cut carefully. Put up the excess paper with the symbol cut out of it as well as the symbol cut. The positive and negative shapes add variety and you get more from each piece of paper.*

INEXPENSIVE COLORED PAPER

When doing lots of cut-outs such as Valentine hearts, Christmas wreaths, or halloween pumpkins, rather than using construction paper, spray paint cheap newsprint the colors that you desire.

—Roseanne and Britt Ripley, Mesa, Arizona

Variations: *Speckling the newsprint with poster paint also gives a nice effect.*

REUSABLE INVESTMENTS

Cheesecloth is lightweight and multi-functional. It can be used to create drop ceilings, tents, clouds, etc. in the cultural hall. Good prices can be arranged from textile wholesalers. Cutting the cloth into ten forty-eight foot panels, with each end glued to a 1″ PVC pipe makes for easy rolled-up storage. Cheesecloth can be dyed and repeatedly bleached and re-dyed different colors.

Small white Christmas lights can be purchased when they go on sale and used throughout the year to decorate inside and outside. Strands can be taped to walls to form trees, city skyline, lightening bolts, arrows, hearts and other objects. Being lightweight, they can be swaged chandelier-like from the high ceiling of a cultural hall and tied off with wire to the walls to create a drop ceiling or dropped to the floor to create a cone or Christmas tree like effect. Laid on top of a cheesecloth "cloud" they become a sky full of twinkling stars. Around a stage front of backdrop they create an air of show biz.

—Richard Maycock, Roswell, Georgia

★ BRING-A-ROLL DECORATIONS

Have everyone bring a roll of toilet paper to the activity and as an ice-breaker, let everyone T.P. the gym. The decorations have not cost anything, the decorating becomes part of the activity and, best of all, the clean up is easy and fast.

—Gary Nelson, California

Variations: *Use colored toilet paper to decorate the cultural hall. Drape toilet paper to cover large areas and hang balloons at the end of each streamer.*

—Joy and Gary Lundburg, Provo, Utah

★ TISSUE PAPER

Using colored tissue paper can bring a lot of color and atmosphere at little cost. They can be spread out on tables, cut up as confetti, stuffed in sacks as centerpieces and even hung at angles and overlapped to create designs on the walls.

—Melody Holland, Kailua, Hawaii

Variations: *Cut the letters of your theme out of the paper and use the left overs to cut up as confetti and spread on table tops to add color.*

★ MAKE YOUR OWN SPOTLIGHT

Most 35-mm slide projectors (the kind that are sitting in most ward libraries) can be adapted to function as a spot light by cutting a hole in the center of a two-inch-square metal aperture plate or a stiff paper and inserting it in the projector as you would a slide. The light beam which shines through the opening in the plate can be focused on a subject or actor the same as when projecting slides on a screen. The size and shape of the hole which is cut is up to the user. Colors may be added by holding a colored plastic sheet in front of the lens of the projector.

—Arnold J. Gregrich, Tooele, Utah, Ensign, *October, 1981, p.62*

★ RUBBER STAMPS

Any inexpensive white disposable table covering can be made more decorative with a rubber stamp and ink pad. Choose a stamp and color that go along with your theme. Using the same stamps on napkins or paper plates personalizes them and creates a dynamite impression for very little money.

—Keith and Teresa Ramsey, Burley, Idaho

Variations: *Cut a potato in two and carve out a design. Dip the potato in poster paint and you have a hand made stamp that could make decorating part of the activity.*

★ EVERYBODY BRINGS SOMETHING

Have everyone bring things from home that go along with the theme to decorate the room in a very personal way. Try filling the room with stuffed animals, old quilts, something handmade, favorite table cloth, most formal dress, etc.

—Jon and Julie Vogl, Milwaukee, Wisconsin

Variations: *People could be asked to bring something of a different color, size, shape, or just something funny like an old shoe or white elephant-type item.*

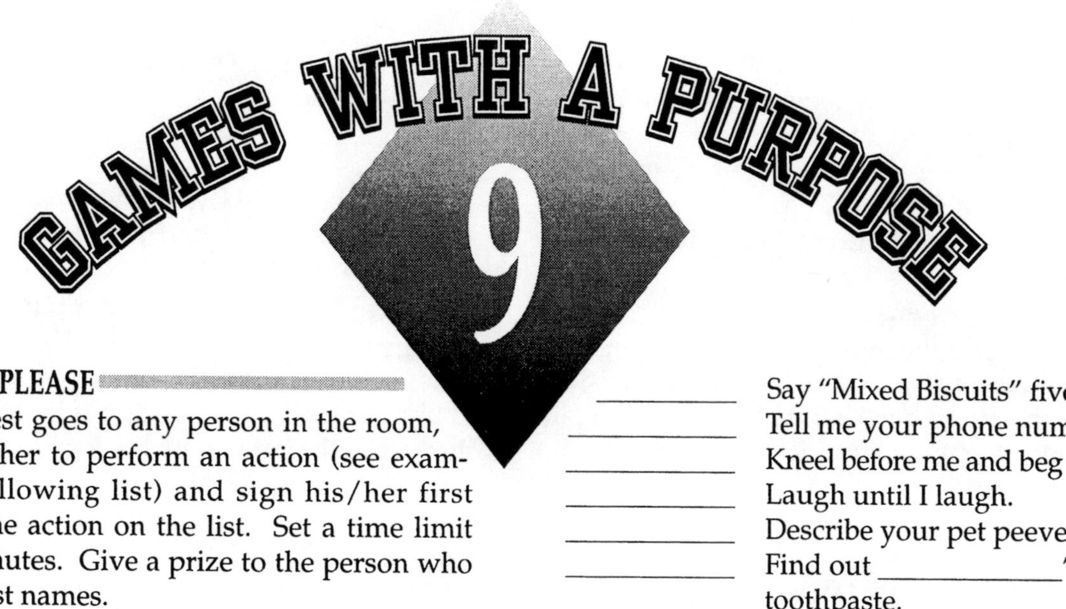

ACTION PLEASE

Each guest goes to any person in the room, and asks him/her to perform an action (see examples on the following list) and sign his/her first name beside the action on the list. Set a time limit such as ten minutes. Give a prize to the person who obtains the most names.

Name:

____________ Whistle "Yankee Doodle" for me.
____________ Give me the time and date.
____________ Do a do-si-do with ____________.
____________ Tell me off while smiling.
____________ Do a tap dance for me.
____________ Compliment me for one minute.
____________ Say "Mixed Biscuits" five times.
____________ Tell me your phone number.
____________ Kneel before me and beg like a dog.
____________ Laugh until I laugh.
____________ Describe your pet peeve.
____________ Find out ____________'s favorite toothpaste.
____________ Salute me and say, "Private (name) reporting sir/ma'am.
____________ Tell me why you're romantic.
____________ Waltz with me.
____________ Introduce ____________ to me.
____________ Bow (or curtsy) three times to me.
____________ Recite the alphabet backwards.

—From Party Starters and Quiet Games, *by Alma Heaton, Bookcraft, 1971, p.16*

ANIMAL FARM

In this mingle game, announce that all those whose birthdays fall from January to March are the "cows." (Ask them *not* to raise their hands or do anything that would reveal the group to which they belong). April through June are "pigs," July through September are "dogs," and October through December are "chickens." Now ask the group to find the others in their birthday group using only the sound of the animal they've been assigned. This will divide the group quickly into four, and will mix people from different stakes or wards. (It will also make a lot of noise!)

MOTHER GOOSE ARITHMETIC

Divide into two teams, each team must create a test for the opposite team using numbers from mother goose rhymes, for example, take the number of blackbirds baked in a pie divided by the number of fiddlers old King Cole had, or take the number of pigs in this little pig went to market times the number of men in a tub. This idea could easily be adapted to scriptures or church related subjects, for example, take the number of temples in Utah minus the number of men in a bishopric.

—Mary Lois Gunnell, Orem, Utah

BALLOON BLOW

Teams are selected with between 20-30 members in each. Each team is given a balloon and instructed to keep the balloon up in the air without using heads, shoulders or hands. To do this, the group must huddle close together and all must try to blow at the balloon to keep it in the air. The team that keeps the balloon up the longest wins.

BALLOON STOMP

Each participant is given a string and a balloon and instructed to blow up the balloon and tie it to his or her ankle. On the "GO" signal, everyone is instructed to try to stomp on each others balloon. The last person that has a balloon tied to his or her ankle is the winner.

Variations: *Play the same game with teams. Blue balloons versus red balloons for example.*

★ GENERAL CONFERENCE BINGO

Keep young children involved by making a bingo card with pictures of things that appear or are talked about during General Conference. Include things like prophet, apostles, Relief Society, service, missionaries, Book of Mormon, Jesus, faith, etc.

—*(This idea appeared in* The Friend.*)*

★ MINGLE BINGO

Make bingo cards leaving the space inside the squares blank. Each person is to fill each blank on their bingo card with three things: someone else's name, ward (or stake, or city), and something unique about them. The person asking the questions will write this information on one of the blank squares in his or her bingo card. This continues until everyone has "filled" cards with different names and information. Use a registration list and start calling out names. When people get a "bingo" they stand and introduce those whose names formed the bingo on their card. (For smaller groups allow everyone a few "free" spaces before filling in the other squares.)

★ BLOW PING PONG

Have several people sit in a circle and hold up a sheet or blanket. A ping pong ball is placed in the middle and each player tries to blow the ball off the sheet. If the ball falls off the sheet over your shoulder you're out. Continue play until you find a winner.

—David L. Bytheway, Murray, Utah

★ OVER-THE-SHOULDER BUCKET BRIGADE

Participants are seated on the grass in a straight line with each person between the knees of the person behind. Each person holds a paper cup. The first person fills her cup from a bucket of water and pours its contents over her shoulder into the cup of the person behind her, who, in turn, passes it on to the next person, and so on until whatever water remains at the end of the line is poured into another bucket. The game is made much more interesting and challenging if all participants are blindfolded. The value of the sense of touch and spoken communication is amplified in an interesting way, and is particularly pointed when cold water is spilled down someone's neck and back! The team with the most water in the end bucket wins.

—Ted and Shirlene Hindmarsh, Provo, Utah

CHARADES

Divide the group into two teams and have one team pick a song, book, movie or slogan that someone in the other team must "act out" well enough that his team mates can identify the song or book from his actions and not from any words. Time limits can be imposed and hand signals can be predetermined to mean certain things: syllable, "sounds like," correct guess, etc. Limiting the charades to church related songs, books, movies and slogans can provide more challenge and instruction.

—*The Activity Book*, LDS, 1977, p.77

Variations: Be *the object! Instead of acting out the words or name of the object, be the object! What fun it is to watch as people try to be a microwave oven, a record player or a curling iron!*

COLORS

Call out a common color and everyone has to touch something that color. Those who don't make it are excluded as you decrease the number of players, or all can continue to play. This is a good mixer game.

—Pat Rosenbury, Misawa, Japan

Variations: *Add other things to touch like wood, metal or glass.*

COME FOLLOW ME

In a park, canyon meadow, or field, blindfold members of the group and instruct them not to talk. Separate them and tell them to locate different objects that are soft, round, hard, big, etc. After they have worked on that assignment for a while, someone, about twenty-five yards away starts singing, "Come Follow Me." Everyone will move toward the voice. Once there, tell them that some of the others have not yet made it to the voice with them. Instruct the group to find and/or help the others. When everyone has gathered, take off the blindfolds, talk about why we're here on earth, following Christ and gathering lost sheep. End by singing the song, "Come Follow Me" again.

—Robin Gunnell, Orem, Utah

COMMON SCENTS

Prepare in advance about ten paper bags prominently numbered on the outside. Inside each, place an aromatic substance—mustard, pepper, vinegar, a rose, or a common perfume such as lilac, etc. Liquids can be placed in small open containers. Scrunch each bag near the top so that it is open just enough to allow the scent to escape—not enough for anyone to see inside. As each guest arrives give him or her a paper and pencil. Walk around the room letting each guest sniff the contents of the small paper bags. He or she should write down the number of the bag and his or her guess as to what it contains. The person with the largest number of correct guesses, wins.

—Party Starters and Quiet Games, *by Alma Heaton, Bookcraft, 1971, p.17*

THE CONFERENCE GAME

During General Conference, or any major Church meeting, have participants write down interesting points from each speaker's ideas, then make up questions based on each talk. Play a game using those questions to refresh everyone's memory and help them internalize the messages.

—Ada Carol Steenhock, Downey, California, Ensign, *March, 1984, p.67*

THE COOPERATION GAME

(For traveling with small children)

Decorate a large, shirt-size box and fill it with sundry items such as gum, small balls, coloring books, a coin purse, a marble bag, etc. This is the Cooperation Store. Label some play money, "cooperation dollars." During long distance travel, "pay" your children for their cooperation and positive attitudes. If some misbehave, do not take dollars away. Simply do not "pay" the misbehavers. As the children earn dollars they can shop at the cooperation store.

—Cheryl Linford, Fruit Heights, Utah, Ensign, *July, 1981, p.53*

DOG AND CAT

Hide peanuts, divide into two teams, the "cats" and the "dogs" (or whatever team names you decide). Have each team elect a team leader. The groups scatter to find the peanuts. When a dog finds one, he stands in place and barks until his team leader collects it. Each cat must meow until his or her team leader collects the peanuts. This contini-ues until they're all found.

—Mary Lois Gunnell, Orem, Utah

Variations: *Use other animals or other objects to find. Have those who find the object(s) stand and sing a song.*

ELBOW TAG

This is an outdoor game of action, running and fun. Have the entire group form a large circle. Tell everyone to find one partner, with whom they will interlock elbows. The only way to be "safe" in this game is if you are locked elbows with one partner. When everyone has their partner, find two individuals who will volunteer to be a chaser and a chasee ("it" and "not it"). In this game, either you are locked with one other player, or you are a chaser or a chasee. The chaser runs after the chasee who will try to become safe by locking elbows with someone in one of the couples before being touched by the chaser. When the chasee locks elbows with someone, for an instant, that couple will become a trio. The person on the other side of the couple from where the chasee "linked," must run away and he or she becomes the new chasee. If the chaser touches the chasee before the chasee "links up," their roles reverse and the chasee becomes chaser. Hints: Make sure there is space between all the couples so it's easy to see places to link up—also, make a rule that the chasee must stay within the circle.

INDOOR GAME NIGHT

Organize different stations throughout the cultural hall to play games like Pictionary, Chutes and Ladders, Candyland, Dominoes, etc. Everybody rotates to a new station at a chosen time interval, or just a few rotate and meet new people at each station.

OUTDOOR GAME NIGHT

Organize a few outdoor game stations with games such as croquet, horseshoes, badminton, volleyball, etc. Rotate at a chosen time interval.

GAMES WITH HOUSEHOLD ITEMS

Balloons:

Relay by running to a distant chair, picking up the balloon, blowing it up and sitting on it until it pops.

Couples run to chair, blow and tie the balloon, place it between them and hug until the balloon pops.

All in a group try to keep their balloons bouncing in the air or use the balloon as an indoor volleyball.

Put the balloon to a distant basket by carrying the balloon with two yardsticks or dowel sticks.

Half-Pint Bottle of Beans:

Drop beans in pop bottles from standing position or toss them into a can or onto a calendar, target, or answer chart on the floor.

Use beans as checkers in egg separators from egg cases.

Start your evening by giving everyone a bean. Player approaches another, an unknown number of beans concealed in his hand; says, "odd or even?" Other player guesses. If right, he must give the questioner the number held.

Use as place markers in Bingo or board games.

See how many you can pick up during a time limit using gloved hands, chop sticks, or measuring spoons.

Bean Bags:

Toss them at each other without dropping or at a target on the floor, wall, or ceiling.

Balancing the bags can be a challenge. Try different areas of the body.

Variations on the Hot potato theme.

Buttons:

Toss, hide, pass or use to decorate something else or as markers, money, or movers in other games.

Variations on button-button, who's got the button theme.

Number Cubes (Dice):

Make your own using wood blocks or sugar cubes. Print numbers or spell the family name or the name of your guest.

Math games (odd or even, closest team to 100 without going over, get to 50 with your rolls using addition, subtraction, multiplication, division or just one of those, etc.).

Drapery Hooks:

Stick them into a cardboard easel or pattern board and toss rubber jar rings at them. Paint number scores, letters, or tic-tac-toe patterns and then toss rings to add scores, spell words, etc.

Marbles:

Roll them, toss them in different targets or hide them.

Raise the vacuum cleaner pipe (or gift-wrap rolls) at one end and put marbles in the chute, catching them at the bottom with a can or in a target.

Metal Washers:

Toss into egg cartons

Newspapers:

Use in a relay where each team is given two newspapers. Individuals take turns traveling a given distance, shifting the papers alternately ahead of them, and stepping only on the papers.

Targets for beans, or marbles.

Cut out words, letters, or pictures to make silly stories or cards.

Paper Plates:

Toss them through a wire coat hanger hung in an open doorway.

Make masks, hats, or use as lily pads in relays

Pop Bottles:

Push with a stick for a relay.

Use to collect beans or match sticks.

Toss rubber jar rings over them from a distance.

Variations on spin the bottle.

Rope or String:

Make a circle of rope where the group tries to conceal the knot while moving it around.

Swing or hang a bean bag or pinata

Use to mark boundaries and starting lines for toss games and relays.

Spoons:

Carry ping pong balls or eggs.

Snap or catapult a ball or bean at a target.

Spoon cotton balls, rice or water from one tin plate to another.

Put out one less spoon than you have players and after a question or signal, everyone grabs.

Tin Cans:

Set up your own miniature golf (or fingernail

golf) with the cans on their sides.

Blindfolded player must stack them as a pyramid, largest can at base.

Target or collection place for beans, washers or balls.

—*Shirley and Monroe Paxman,* Family Night Fun, *1963, pp.145-151*

GUESS WHAT IS INSIDE

Wrap up different objects in boxes (raw egg, banana, corn flakes, etc.) and then by shaking or smelling the box, the one on the spot must guess what is inside.

—*Keith and Teresa Ramsey, Burley, Idaho*

HULA HOOP RELAY

Divide the group into equal teams of about fifty (or less). Split each team in half and have them form two straight lines facing each other from opposite ends of the playing area. In the middle of the space between each team (about 50 feet), have someone hold up a hula hoop. As the race begins, the first person in one line runs through the hula hoop to the other line of people on his or her team. He or she grabs the hand of the first person in line, and the two of them run again through the hula hoop back to the first line, where one more person joins them. Then they run back to get a fourth person and so on, until their whole team is hand in hand and they all run through the hoop.

HUMAN TREASURE HUNT

Everyone is given a list of things to find among the others in the group (an example is printed below). Have the person who meets the criteria sign on the line following the statement.

1. Find someone who has the same birth month as you have. ______________
2. Find someone your own age. ______________
3. Find someone with brown hair. ______________
4. Find someone who's been to Hawaii. ________
5. Find someone who is 6′ 0″ tall. ______________

You can make as many or as few as you like, and you can invent criteria to meet the characteristics of your group.

—*See also* Party Starters and Quiet Games, *by Alma Heaton, Bookcraft, 1971, p.6*

KNOTS

This game is played in teams of between ten and twenty. Each team forms a circle facing inward. At the "GO" signal, participants of each team run to the middle of the circle and grab the hand of another team member. Each participant should have grabbed the hand of two different team members (one in each hand). As soon as all of the hands have been connected the team begins to untangle the knot. The first team to do so wins.

GREAT LAP SIT

This game is played with the whole group as one big team. The group forms a big circle facing inward. Then they all turn to the right so that they are facing the back of the person on their right. Then they put their hands on the shoulders of the persons in front of them. On the count of three, the group is instructed to sit down slowly on the lap of the person behind them, saying "Sit on my knees please." It will become immediately apparent that in order to accomplish this feat, the group must be standing very close together. It may take two or three tries to do it successfully.

Variations: *If you are successful, try taking steps. "One, two three right foot! One, two three, left foot! etc.*

MINGLE

Appoint someone to be "voice" (someone with a loud voice or a microphone). The rest of the group gathers close together, and waits for the voice to call a number (between one and ten). When the number is called, five for example, everyone in the group must "mingle" into groups of five, put their arms around each others shoulders and sit down. Those failing to get into a group of five must move outside the playing area and watch the rest of the game. Numbers are called until only two remain. To make this a mingling game, ask each group to introduce themselves to the others as they sit down and wait for the next number is called.

MUSICAL KNEES

Have all the boys in the room kneel down in a circle and the girls walk around the circle as long as there is music playing. When the music stops, all the girls must sit on a knee. The one who doesn't find a knee is out. Then, one of the boys is removed and the game continues. Good mixer, ice-breaker, or dance activity.

—Dale Capener, Yukoska, Japan

Variations: *Try passing paper sacks that are placed over heads from person to person during music.*

MUSICAL SPORTS

Choose a sport (Volleyball) or game (Badminton) that will involve the whole group. Have several different games going at once. Play music during the game. Follow the normal rules with one addition: each time the music stops everyone must freeze. Fastest team to freeze receives extra points. The music starts again and the game picks up from where it left off.

INDOOR OLYMPICS

Hold a series of indoor games. Some activities might include: Discus throw, using a paper plate. Shot put, with securely tied, blown-up paper bags or balloons. Javelin throw, using a plastic drinking straw. Fifty-yard dash, blowing a ping-pong ball or cotton ball a designated distance. Relay, using two foot-sized pieces of cardboard. One person "runs" by hopping from one piece of cardboard to the next, while his partner moves the pieces into place as fast as he can.

—Dian Thomas, Provo, Utah, Ensign, *February, 1981, p.60. See also* The Activity Book, *LDS, 1977, "Mock Track Meet" p.125.*

PARTNERS

At the beginning of the evening (conference, dance), pair everyone with a partner. Periodically during the evening, pound a big gong. From wherever they are, all partners must come back together and sit down. The last couple down has their names put on a big list. Activities resume as normal until the gong is pounded again. At the end of the evening names are chosen from the list to do some something silly or some odd job to clean up. This idea can be adapted to larger groups by assigning everyone an original group (Nephites, Lamanites, Jaredites, etc.) so everyone is assigned a group rather than a partner; when the gong is hit they must reunite with their group. Stragglers names are put on the list. This is a good way to get everyone's attention for announcements or instructions throughout the dance or conference.

—Mary Lois Gunnell, Orem, Utah

PEOPLE PIZZA PUZZLE

This game gets people to mingle in a puzzling way! Make a large circular pizza out of cardboard and cut it into jigsaw puzzle type pieces (about thirty). If you have, say, 150 people at the activity, you could make five pizzas out of different colors of poster board. Cut the pizza into pieces, and give one piece to each person as they enter the activity. The first challenge is to find the people in the room with a piece of the same color, the second challenge is to put the entire pizza together with the other thirty people and their pieces. The object of the game is to complete your group's pizza first. Lots of fun no matter how you slice it. Call it the Peter Piper Pepperoni People Pizza Puzzle!

> **Variations:** *To fit the theme of your activity, make the puzzle in the shape of a jack-o-lantern, turkey, or Christmas tree.*

"PLUG THE SIEVE" WATER GAME

Working against the clock, teams shuttle buckets of water to fill a plastic 60 gallon garbage container which has been perforated with twenty or thirty half-inch diameter holes up and down its sides. Two or three members shuttle the water buckets while the remaining team members plug the holes with fingers, toes, elbows, chins, or anything else they can get to fit. The team that can fill it to overflowing in the shortest time wins.

—Ted and Shirlene Hindmarsh, Provo, Utah

PYRAMIDS

This is a very fast and fun game. The group is divided into smaller groups of 10 each. On the "GO" signal each team is instructed to build a four level pyramid as fast as possible. The first team to do so wins.

RED LIGHT, GREEN LIGHT

Find an area with obstacles, like trees or bushes, or create your own in the gym with overturned tables and chairs making it difficult to walk through in a straight line (if you use a gym, turn out the lights). Don't allow the participants to see the obstacle area. Gather the youth together in one place and the adult leaders together in another place. Explain to the youth group that in order for the game to work, they must not peek out of their blindfolds and they must be quiet. Tell them the object of the game is to move towards the voice. The rules of the game are:

1. Listen only to the voice saying "red light" and "green light."
2. Go forward on "green light," stop on "red light."

Only give the rules once (that's part of the game). Tell the adult leaders the rules the youth have been told. Tell the adults that their job is to be the adversary (a fact of which the youth are not aware). When the youth are halfway through the obstacles, the adults should approach them, and with soothing voices, whisper to the youth things like, "You've done enough, you can sit down here," or "The real way to win is to go to the corner," or "I don't want you to get hurt so stop here." Some of the youth will forget the rules and follow the adults' misleading counsel. Others will remember the rules and proceed to the voice no matter how hard the adults try to dissuade them. When it looks like things have run their course, stop the game and ask everyone to remove the blindfolds. Ask all the youth to come up to the front and begin a discussion. Have the youth make comments about what happened and why. Lead the discussion and let them come up with their own analogies and how this game relates to life and the struggles of the world.

Variations: *Divide the youth group in half. Tell one half they are members of the church. Instead of the "red light green light" voice, tell the youth there will be a rope which will lead them to heaven. Tell them the way to pray is to raise their hand. Have only one adult "answer" the prayers (it needs to be one recognizable voice). The rope is placed through the room intertwined with the obstacles. Tell the other half only "This is life" and give them no further clues. As they progress or give up, you can whisper in their ears, "What do you do when life gets hard?" If they say, "You pray," tell them, "The way you pray in this room is to raise your hand." The assigned voice can* *then give them instructions. Use the analogy that the rope is the iron rod or the scriptures, and that the scriptures and prayer will help us return to Heavenly Father.*

—Nathan Pinnock, Salt Lake City, Utah

RELAY RACES

A good old fashioned relay race never fails. Use your creativity. Have teams do things such as fill a glass a teaspoon at a time, or run to a typewriter and type their full name three times without a mistake, or chew up a soda cracker and then blow up a balloon. Or have them recite a scripture or a tongue twister. There's no limit to the different kinds of things you can do in a relay.

RUN TO THE ANSWER

As you review main points of a lesson, post signs around the room with the answers on them or simply "A," "B," and "C" in different corners for some multiple choice questions. Ask a question, give time to think, and then say, "go!" All must run to the answer they believe is correct. Signs can be posted on walls, floors or even outside for larger groups. Rather than worrying about children's short attention spans, use this type of an idea to pick up the pace and involve their bodies in movement and learning. It's a fun idea to use with adults too in more casual settings.

—Dianne Dibb Forbis, Rexburg, Idaho, Ensign, *April, 1982, p.65*

SIMPLE THINGS

Don't overlook the simple things. Play kick-the-can, or hide-and-seek. Hold a tiddlewink tournament, play jacks or hopscotch, play frisbees in the park. Add a new twist to any of the old standards for more excitement. Imagine trying to play hide-and-seek in the dark when each player has an illuminated flashlight attached to their leg!

SIT-DOWN SCAVENGER HUNT

Give each participant an old catalog or magazine, a pair of scissors, and an envelope to organize his "finds." Then give each a list of ten to fifteen specific items to find. If you're dealing with non-readers, use pictures.

—Dian Thomas, Provo, Utah, Ensign, *February, 1981, p.60*

SOUND-A-NARY

Divide the players into several small groups. Pick three or four people to be the guessers (use adult leaders or chaperons). Give each group a piece of paper which tells them what they're supposed to "be." The group is to make the sounds or the noise of the thing written on the paper so the guessers can guess it. Someone is assigned to be a timer, and he or she will listen while the guessers shout out their guesses. The group which helps the guessers to get the answer quickest wins. (Use things like a jungle, a city, a football game, a zoo, a library, etc.)

BOOK OF MORMON SPELLING BEE

Hold a spelling bee using names of Book of Mormon prophets and places. See the pronunciation guide in the back of the book.

Variations: *Try the same idea with the Old and New Testaments, The Pearl of Great Price, etc. Or, have a spelling bee using the names of the current General Authorities or Latter-day prophets.*

SPIN THE BOTTLE WITH A TWIST

Sit in a circle and play spin the bottle. When the bottle points your way, you must say something nice about the person to your right or you must quickly do a small act of service for him or her (make a bed, wash a window, polish a shoe).

—Jolene Richmond, Renton, Washington

SPONGE TOSS

This game requires the following equipment: leg ties, big sponges, a water container, water and a rope. This is a relay type race. Players on each team are paired off. The first pair stand back-to-back and use the leg ties to tie their ankles. They interlock arms and one player receives the sponge and they begin to walk toward the rope. When they reach the rope, the player with the sponge throws the sponge over the rope and the other player must catch it before they can return to the starting line. When the first pair does return to the starting line the leg ties are exchanged and the next pair starts toward the rope. The first team to finish wins.

STAND UP

This game is played in pairs. Each pair is seated on the ground back to back. They lock arms and on the "GO" signal they attempt to stand up without using their arms. The first pair to do this wins.

STATUE TOGETHERNESS

Teams stack themselves onto a round wooden disk that is only two feet in diameter. Once they get into place, they hang on by whatever means they can, and sing as many primary songs as they can remember all the way through. The team that can sing the most primary songs while still holding on, wins.

—Ted and Shirlene Hindmarsh, Provo, Utah

STICK PULLING

Sit down facing a partner with the soles of your feet against your partner, both holding an old broom handle or straight stick, try to pull your opponent over to your side or get him or her off balance. This game was a favorite of Joseph Smith.

THINK HARD OR HARDLY THINK

Gather the following objects. Each object should be numbered and displayed on a table easily accessible to everyone. As each guest arrives give him a paper like the following and have him fill in the blanks. Guests must find the object on the table which represents the numbered article, and write it in the blank.

Article:

1. "K" written on a piece of paper
2. Calendar
3. Two banana peels
4. A match floating in a cup of water
5. Sixteen pieces of candy
6. Toothbrush
7. Water "pitcher"
8. A can of "sage" seasoning
9. Candle
10. Salt
11. Fork
12. Taxes (carpet tacks)
13. Buttercup (butter in a cup)
14. "N" written on a piece of paper
15. Stamp
16. Dictionary

17. Sponge
18. A pair of dice on some earth
19. Iron

Answers:

1. End of pork
2. A bunch of dates
3. A pair of slippers
4. A swimming match
5. Sweet sixteen
6. Never borrowed, never lent
7. Seen at a ball game
8. A wise man
9. Out for the night
10. The ending of a Bible character
11. Branching off a river
12. One of the causes of the American Revolution
13. A spring flower
14. The end of ambition
15. Ready to be licked
16. Where to find happiness
17. An absorbing subject
18. A paradise on earth
19. Birthplace of Burns

—Party Starters and Quiet Games, *by Alma Heaton, Bookcraft, 1971, p.22*

TOILET PAPER MUMMIES

Given several rolls of toilet paper, groups must mummify someone in their group or a selected leader. There is a time limit and you should set a distance that they all have to run to get to the one who has been selected as the mummy. If groups are competing, the mummy who is best covered wins.

—Joan Salgy, Orem, Utah

TRAVEL GAMES

Whenever activities involve travel (temple trips, etc.) and group discussion gives way to boredom, try these car games:

- Draw a bingo card and write the names of things you'll pass along the way.
- See how many out of state license plates you can identify. Extra points for knowing the capitol city of the state.
- Make words or sentences using the letters of the license plates on the cars you see, or math problems using the numbers.
- Go through the alphabet finding the letters on billboards and roadsigns. Make it more challenging by using first letters of words.

- Divide the car down the middle. Decide what you're looking for: Cows, a 7-11 store, a certain make of car, signs etc. The first team to identify one of these gets a point. You can also arrange a way for a team to lose points—which side of the car a cemetery is on, etc.

—Beth Duering, Salt Lake City, Utah

★ THE TRUST FALL

Participants stand erect on a platform (elevated four feet from ground level), their fingers clutching the seams of their trousers, and tip backward into the waiting arms of the others who catch them. Even though the danger level is low, tipping backward requires ultimate trust in your team. An interesting sensation that is much more difficult than it sounds, but is profoundly satisfying once accomplished.

—Ted and Shirlene Hindmarsh, Provo, Utah

★ FEATHER VOLLEYBALL

Tie a string between two chairs to serve as a net. All players are on their knees. The object is to work together as a team to blow the feather across the string to the other team.

—Robin Gunnell, Debbie Hawkins, Orem, Utah

★ ONE SHOT WATER FIGHT

Place a tub or bucket of water in the middle of the back yard and make it so that is the only source of ammunition. Give everyone a cup the same size. The game ends when the tub is empty.

—The Walker family, May Creek, Washington

★ WHAT'S THE TRUTH?

As people in the group are introduced, they must say several interesting things about themselves. The group decides which comments are true and which are not.

—Jon and Julie Vogl, Milwaukee, Wisconsin

Variations: *Have each person write on a piece of paper one unusual thing that they have done which is true. The player must include their name on the paper. The moderator picks a piece of paper from among those submitted and* *chooses three people (one of whom is the real author). These three describe in further detail what happened to them (two are bluffing). After the three have told their story, the rest of the group votes on who they think is telling the truth.*

HUMAN TYPEWRITER

Assign each member of the group a different letter. As questions are asked, answers must be spelled out by having the people stand and call out their letters or hold up a card with the letter on it.

—Jennifer Johnston, Bartlesville, Oklahoma

Variations: *Try giving questions or answers in Braille or Morse Code. Invent your own codes and send messages from group to group or try to identify common scripture verses quickly.*

SPOONS

On tables or on the floor, provide one less spoon than participants gathered. As questions are asked, players must grab spoons. The one person left over must then attempt to answer the question. This makes for a fast-paced and engaging review session.

Variations: *Divide the whole group into teams and keep track of points.*

ACTIVITY TIME

Set aside a regular time after breakfast or lunch as "activity time." Officially open with a song and prayer and then color, play games, braid yarn, or write a letter to a grandparent. Having activities at a set time lets me schedule my day easier and gives the children something to look forward to. They can be more patient when you're doing dishes or working on a project when you can say, "Activity time is coming."

—Judith Rose Barrett, Havre, Montana, Ensign, *February, 1983, p.63*

Variations: *Arrange a set reading time, journal time, scripture story time. Togetherness Time: Create a poster with a large clock face on it. At the top are the words, "Time for . . ." and on the clock face are the names of all the children in the family. Below the paper clock are pictures of activities parents can do with children: Sit and talk, Visit the library, Go to the park, Read books, Play games, Bake, Draw, Mold clay, Sew, Dress up, Sing, Build, Throw Balls, Tramp, Swing, Write in a journal, etc. During the course of the day, the clock can point to special time for each child in which he can select an activity to do with mom or dad. If you're feeling especially pressed, set a timer to limit the activity. This is one way to make sure you're getting some valuable one-on-one time with each child every day.*

—Lorie N. Davis, Southfield, Michigan, Ensign, *October, 1983, p.59*

ANCESTOR PUPPET-TREE

Start by making a big family tree, about six feet high and seven feet wide, of thick plywood or cardboard. Then, make puppets to represent four generations of your ancestors. The puppets can be made from oatmeal boxes, cans, fake fur, and fabric scraps. By positioning yourself behind the tree you can operate the puppets' mouths as they tell the story of their lives and interact with each other.

—*Dale Hardman, Kensington, Maryland,* Ensign, *July, 1985, p.69*

Variations: *Rather than puppets, have children dress in something from the time period of each ancestor of focus or hold something that belonged to him or her.*

APPRECIATION POCKETS

Everyone prepares his own pocket out of paper or fabric and can decorate it as he wishes. Then, to go into these "mailboxes" every member of the family is given papers with the names of the other members of the family at the top. Everyone is to write a note telling something he appreciates about the others in his family and slip it in respective pockets.

—*Shoemaker Family, Sunnyside, Washington*
(Adapted from the 1971 Family Home Evening Manual)

Variations: *Slip the notes in people's shoes or under pillows or try to out guess them and leave it in a place you know they will be that day (maybe the cookie jar or a box of favorite breakfast cereal).*

MEMORIZE ARTICLES OF FAITH

By going over an Article of Faith every time you kneel for regular family prayer, even young children will be able to memorize them. The method is painless and doesn't require any extra effort or time.

—*Elizabeth Martinsen, Provo, Utah,* Ensign, *August, 1984, p.70*

Variations: *Memorize sayings, a family motto, theme, quotes, or songs. As you read Bible and Book of Mormon stories to your children, pick a pertinent scripture from one of the stories as your scripture of the week. Look it* *up, repeat it several times, talk about what it means, who is talking, and the circumstances around that particular scripture. Copy, or have the children copy, the scripture onto a brightly colored piece of construction paper and post it on the refrigerator. Each night at dinner, children can earn stars to place on the poster by reciting the scripture or answering questions about it.*

—Marlene A. Sullivan, Roosevelt, Utah,
Ensign, *July, 1983, p.55*

HYMNS AT HOME

Make hymn practice a regular part of your Sunday routine. Learn an unfamiliar hymn or memorize a favorite. Work just one verse at a time. This way, hymns become more familiar to everyone in the family and their messages can be better internalized.

—Linda Garner, Sandy, Utah, Ensign, *June, 1988, p.69*

Variations: *Sing a hymn before family prayer, offer motivation for memorizing additional verses. Find out more about those who wrote the hymns.*

A SONG IN YOUR HOME

Make music a part of your family time by learning, singing and teaching with Church Songs. Greet Dad with, "I'm so glad when Daddy Comes Home." Replace a lengthy lecture with, "Quickly, I'll Obey." Break up a family argument with "Love at Home." End a long family night lesson with "The Time is Far Spent" and tuck children in with "My Heavenly Father Loves Me."

—Laurie Williams Sowby, American Fork, Utah,
Ensign, *March, 1985, p.71*

AWARDS BANQUET

Set an evening aside when you prepare a special dinner. Have everyone in the family dress up in their nice clothes. After the formal dinner, present awards to each member of the family. These can be for accomplishments in school or scouts, or focus on more personal accomplishments, as in help around the house or quiet acts of service that have been noticed. If you make the awards evening a yearly event, you could video the awards from year to year and create a fun and formal addition to your family history.

—Scott and Angel Anderson, Bluffdale, Utah

Variations: *Have a different dinner for each member of the family. Let each choose his/her favorite dish and honor each child separately.*

FAMILY HOME CONFERENCE

Select a theme and plan a formal family conference. Start with a formal dinner and have the family members present the talks they have prepared on the conference theme.

—*Eileen Giberson, Amarillo, Texas,* Ensign, *September, 1984, p.68*

Variations: *Have a testimony meeting. Record the occasion on audio or video tape for far-away relatives or as part of your family history. Make this occasion a time for personal interviews and father's blessings. It can also be a good time to review goals.*

BACKYARD CAMP OUT

Pitch your tent right in the backyard. Roast marshmallows over a candle flame.

—*Robin Gunnell, Debbie Hawkins, Orem, Utah*

Variations: *Try a tent in the family room or just set up under blanket-covered card tables. Have a family slumber party on a non-school night. Bed the entire family down in the family or living room. Popcorn and scary stories make it feel like a real slumber party. Turn out the lights and use flash lights.*

—*Jan Murphy, Tucson, Arizona,*
Ensign, *January, 1985, p.72*

A BEDTIME CHAT

After baths, teeth brushing, getting drinks, reading stories and prayers, talk with your children about the day. Have each child be silent until it is his turn to chat. Ask, "What was the most fun thing you did today?" to start with and let the chat go from there.

—*Susan Tanner Holmes, Salt Lake City, Utah,*
Ensign, *February, 1988, p.66*

Variations: *Ask thought provoking questions like "If you were an animal, what would you be? If you were a car, what would you be? What color do you feel inside tonight?"*

Sometimes it can bring more of a response than simply reviewing the days events.

JIFFY BOOKS

A Jiffy Book is a modified quiet book and can help keep a child's attention during church meetings and reinforce basic gospel principles. Start with an 8-by-10 inch vinyl photo album in your child's favorite color. The kind with self-adhesive plastic pages works well. Apply sticker cloth straps as handles. Inside, include items such as pictures of Jesus, mother, father, brothers, sisters, grandparents and cousins. You can include pictures of prophets, temples and poems or stories clipped from the *Friend.* Make some of the pages activity oriented.

—Joan H. Evans, Salt Lake City, Utah, Ensign, *April, 1984, p.74*

Variations: *Try having older children make books for younger children in the family. Get together with creative friends and everyone bring an idea and materials for one page in everyone's book. By the time you swap, everyone will have a complete book of shared ideas and materials.*

SUNDAY BOX

Develop a special Sunday Box for your family. Include a list of suggestions for appropriate Sabbath activities. Have supplies of paper, scissors, crayons, glue, envelopes and stamps. When children get bored, pull out the Sunday box. If the box is saved and reserved just for Sundays, children will look forward to using it and it will not become routine.

—Robin Gunnell, Debbie Hawkins, Orem, Utah

READ A BOOK TOGETHER

In place of an hour spent in front of the TV each evening, choose a good book and read a chapter a night together—just like a teacher does in school after lunch.

—Robin Gunnell, Debbie Hawkins, Orem, Utah

Variations: *Tell stories by taking turns or simply start the story and then pass it on to the next person in the family and let them continue it.*

USE BREAKFAST TIME

Lots of things can be accomplished around the

breakfast table: hold mini family councils, take opportunities to teach or listen to scriptures, or review the activities of the day and focus on needs of children. Leave children with a positive feeling for the coming day, and family prayer. Somehow, if you do it at breakfast, it has a better chance of not getting overlooked.

—K. Dean Black, Tucker, Georgia, Ensign, *June, 1985, p.70.*

Variations: *Have a formal devotional. After family scripture study, take five minutes to review articles of faith or memorize scriptures. Then, sing a Church song before you have your family prayer. Exchange hugs and "I love you's" before scurrying off to the hectic activities of the day.*

—Lina Hatch, Gilbert Arizona, Ensign, *March, 1981, p.34.*

For parents and older children who eat on their own, cover the back of the cereal box (the usually breakfast reading material) with something more uplifting—a thought or scripture.

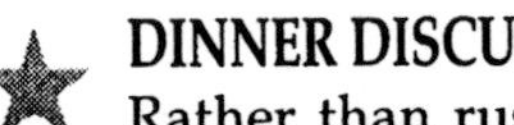

DINNER DISCUSSION

Rather than rushing off after dinner, use the time to talk as a family about what has happened during the day. As time permits, talk about Gospel topics and relate Gospel teachings to the experiences of the day.

—Mark and Michele Gunnell, Fullerton, California

Variations: *Try pulling a topic or question out of a bowl and having everyone express an opinion having to do with the topic. It might be a change of pace to try to guess what different members of the family did during the day.*

FAMILY BULLETIN BOARD

In a central location, post a bulletin board on which you can hang children's school work, pictures of distant relatives, report cards, and notices of upcoming events. You may choose to create a similar show place on the front of your refrigerator with magnets.

Variations: *Instead of using a bulletin board for display, use your table. First, put your prettiest tablecloth on the table. Next, put down anything you might put on a bulletin* *board: quotes, charts, scriptures, children's art work, etc. Finally, cover the table with a piece of heavy, clear plastic. Make sure you've purchased enough to hang several inches over the edges of the table. When it's time to clean up, just wipe the plastic with a damp dishcloth the same way you would any other plastic tablecloth.*

—Sherry L. Simmerman, Penrose, Colorado, Ensign, *June, 1988, p.68*

Variations: *Spotlight different family members throughout the year. This might be especially good for relatives who live far away that you want to keep in mind. Have different children take turns putting together the sharing space.*

CALENDAR HISTORY

Get a medium-sized calendar and begin to record you children's daily accomplishments. Since the space for each day is limited in size, note only the day's highlights. At the end of the month, simply tear off the calendar page and copy it for each child's journal. Then, write a note on the back and send it to Grandma and Grandpa to keep them in touch with family activities.

—Nancy Betts Gorzesik, Raleigh, North Carolina, Ensign, *February, 1984, p.60*

Variations: *Try guessing ahead on a calendar for the year when different things might happen—when a baby will be born or a mission call might come. Predicting and seeing who comes closest increases the anticipation for an up-coming family event.*

A YEAR'S SUPPLY OF GREETING CARDS

Buy greeting cards during the after-holiday sales. Then, at the beginning of each month or year, address and stamp each of them. As time to send draws near, write an appropriate message and mail the cards. No more last-minute running to the store for cards, and no more forgotten birthdays or holidays.

—Susan Turnbull, Portland Oregon, Ensign, *October, 1979, p.63*

Variations: *Reproduce some original designs that your children have come up with.*

A REMINDER BINDER

Get an inexpensive three-ring binder and insert twelve pocket dividers, one for each month of the year. List each months's birthdays and anniversaries on the appropriate pocket and then keep them stocked with low cost cards, envelopes and stamps.

—Denise Wright, Farmington, Missouri, Ensign, *October, 1985, p.59*

NUMBERED CHORES

Number the chores one through six. Then each member of the family rolls a die and does the chore corresponding with that number.

—Keith and Teresa Ramsey, Burley, Idaho

Variations: *Numbers could stand for different parts of a Family Home Evening (Song, Prayer, lesson, talent, etc.) or different places in the car on a longer trip.*

COLLECTIONS

Collecting souvenirs, relics, newspaper clippings, and other momentos of interest to the individual and the family are great ways to spend time together as a family. All these are forms of preserving, reconstructing, and reliving with the interesting and memorable people, places, and experiences in one's life.

—Shirley and Monroe Paxman, Family Night Fun, *1963, p.108*

Variations: *Try stamps, postcards, valentines, greeting and Christmas cards, dance and other programs as well.*

NEIGHBORHOOD COOK OUTS

Let your family be in charge of organizing a cook out for your neighbors. Every child has some sort of responsibility. (Make invitations, deliver invitations, set up, clean up, help serve, entertainment, mingle games, etc.) This can be a fun and unifying activity for the neighborhood. More importantly, it can be a learning experience for the members of your family.

—Val C. Wilcox, Provo, Utah

Variations: *Invite Ward friends, families of children's school friends, children's school teachers.*

CULTURAL HOUR

Every so often, let your Family Home Evening focus on aspects of art and culture. Learn basics about famous authors, composers, and artists. Listen to or see excerpts of their works (available at public libraries) and train children in audience etiquette and proper manners when attending a cultural event.

—Mary Lois Gunnell, Orem, Utah

Variations: *Assign children to present their current favorite groups and music—how interesting it could be!*

TAKE-WHAT-COMES DINNER

The family goes to the store and each is given a small amount of money and a time limit to buy what they would like without going over their given amount. At the ending time, everyone meets, buys what they have selected, goes home and makes a meal out of what ever is there.

—Becky Crockett, Phoenix, Arizona

Variations: *Assign each member of the family a different food group to be in charge of, or limit what can be bought with some rules (you have to get something that starts with the letter of your first name).*

FORMAL DINNERS

Although most dinners are eaten at the kitchen counter, establish the pattern that at least one meal a week (Sunday) is eaten off the formal China in the formal dining room. This allows for good training in dining etiquette (seating the ladies, waiting for the hostess to begin before eating, etc.) and allows for greater responsibilities (setting the table, helping with the cooking, etc.) but most of all, formal dining usually gives the family more time together to talk without the TV or radio blaring in the background.

—Val C. Wilcox, Provo, Utah

Variations: *Set your dining room up like a fancy restaurant and actually have someone seat the family and order from menus. Instead of a tip, have everyone help with dishes.*

LOTS TO DO

Post a list of about thirty no-cost ideas on the refrigerator. When children say there is nothing to do, direct them to the list. The items are written out simply in one or two words, so the child is not limited and must use his imagination in deciding what to do. For instance, "puppets" may send one child in the direction of the toy box, while another may go to the craft supplies. Other items included could be skates, bikes, puzzles, paste, playhouse, tent, play dough, balls, etc. The only rule is that the child must think of something to do. If he makes it clear down the list and still has nothing to do, he must accept the last item on the list: take a nap. It seems no child ever gets that far down the list.

—Karma Lewis and Paula J. Lewis, San Bernadino, California, Ensign, *April, 1981, p.64*

Variations: *Include service oriented items, have children make up lists for each other, Blindfold children and have them pick from the list in pin-the-tail-on-the-donkey style.*

ANYTIME EASTER EGG HUNT

Using plastic eggs, assign each child a certain color of egg or area of the house in which to search. Inside each egg is a message, treat, clue, etc.

—Keith and Teresa Ramsey, Burley, Idaho

Variations: *Hide things that children need to get ready for bed: tooth brush, pajamas, story book, stuffed animal, etc.*

FAMILY ART SHOW

Gather a variety of materials and let everyone in the family create a masterpiece. If no one can think of an idea, you can work around a theme, draw an item that is placed in the center of the room, or illustrate favorite scripture stories. Finished products can be mounted and displayed in the home for a while. Nice work can be saved for journals and personal records.

—Jan Murphy, Tucson, Arizona, Ensign, *January, 1985, p.73*

Variations: *Salt dough sculptures, tooth pick sculptures, these can be made into ornaments.*

Make a traveling art show by trading your artistic work with relatives or friends.

FAMILY FLAG

Create a family flag. Choose shapes, symbols and colors that will mean a lot to your family. Perhaps you can use the letters in your name or all the initials of the members of the family in some creative way. Plan the flag on paper, discussing each part. Create the flag by sewing or gluing fabric scraps together and/or drawing on a cloth with felt markers. Display the flag—permanently or just on special occasions—outside your home or in the family or living room.

—Gerald L. O'Barr, San Diego, California, Ensign, *July, 1985, p.42*

Variations: *Write a family song or select a favorite that you can adopt as yours. Have each child create their own flag or pennant. A family crest or seal could be developed. Choose your own family colors.*

FAMILY SAYINGS AND SLOGANS

Establish little sayings or slogans that will be meaningful to your family and repeated often. For example, during your Family Home Evening, set a chair for each member of the family in a circle. As you discuss the beautiful truths of Temples and sealing powers, say something to the effect that, in the Celestial Kingdom, you want every chair full—no one missing. The lesson will take on added meaning each time the family gather for dinner or any activity where someone happens to be gone. It might take some prompting at first, but soon, even the youngest will catch on and say, "We want every chair full."

—Homer M. and Venita LeBaron, Greensboro, North Carolina

Variations: *Try a family mission statement, motto, or cheer to be repeated on special occasions. These could be lettered nicely for each one to put in his/her bedroom.*

FAMILY PLACE MATS

Have your children draw family oriented pictures and memories on colored poster board with marking pens. Cover the poster board on both top and bottom with contact paper. These can make fun gifts for relatives too.

—*Janet R. Balmforth, Provo, Utah,* Ensign, *April, 1981, p.62*

Variations: *Personalize wall paper, pillow cases, paper plates and cups for a picnic. Try a personalized tablecloth: Using a bed sheet, have members of the family draw or write something in a designated area of the cloth. These can be embroidered to make the cloth more permanent. This way special family days are remembered. It can become a tradition and little family history as it is kept up from year to year. If the cloth is pulled out every Christmas or Thanksgiving, it can become a holiday tradition as well.*

—*Wanda West Badger, Salt Lake City, Utah,* Ensign, *December, 1981, p.65*

★ A FAMILY QUILT

Design your own family quilt. Using fabric crayon, have every member of the family draw pictures. These could be of meaningful family events or memories. Then, using an iron, transfer the drawings onto some natural fiber fabric. This becomes your quilt top. Using quilting frames, tie the quilt and then turn the raw edges of the quilt in and stitch.

—*Candace Smith, Tempe, Arizona,* Ensign, *April, 1976, p.41*

Variations: *Use names and pictures of relatives, family mission statement, scenes from favorite scripture stories, temples and places where family members have served missions, etc.*

★ FAMILY JIGSAW

Draw a family tree and place pictures of family members on their respective branches. Have the completed chart photographed or photocopied and then mount it on heavy cardboard. Use a jigsaw or sharp knife to cut around the various people on the chart. Let children learn to assemble the puzzle, and in the process familiarize themselves with their progenitors.

—*Charlotte Mitchell, Murray, Utah,* Ensign, *December, 1978, p.41*

Variations: *Use pictures of your children, home, pets, favorite family fun spots, places of work, cars, chapel, etc.*

FAMILY GAME CHEST

Family game nights can be fun and lively with the assistance of a homemade game chest. Find an old discarded suitcase and decorate it with your own designs. Then, fill it with materials around the house that can be used for games. All materials should be replaced after using. With proper care, the family will never be without needed materials when there is time for games. You won't have to go through the frustration many families feel when everyone is in the mood for some fun but you don't have the things you need. Try including chalk, pie tins, bean bags, marbles, ping pong balls, straws, clothes pins, string, dominoes, rubber balls, dull knife, empty bottles, paper pads and pencils, timer, balloons, spoons, washers, egg cartons, checkers, chop sticks, etc.

—Shirley and Monroe Paxman, Family Night Fun, *1963, p.144*

Variations: *Keep your family's favorite board games together in an easy-to-reach spot. Have children create their own games or make up new or more complicated rules to old favorites. Rather than spending money on expensive toys, use things that are in your own home to provide a rich and creative environment in which to grow: Dress-up materials such as old gloves, hats, dresses and shoes; kitchen materials such as pots, pans, boxes and cartons. Macaroni can be made into jewelry and beans are great for paper plate rattles or collages; Junk such as spools, cardboard, and bottle lids; Water and earth outside in the yard.*

—Janene Wolsey Baadsgaard, Spanish Fork, Utah,
Ensign, *July, 1984, p.67*

THE GAME OF FAMILY LIFE

Maintain your child's sense of belonging to a larger family by creating a game where the object is to start from your house and travel to visit relatives all across the country. The first to get home wins. Players can advance squares of miles by rolling dice or picking cards (You did a great job cleaning your room . . . advance 5, or, You forgot to feed the cats . . . go back three).

—Katheryn Kleekamp, Bedford, Massachusetts,
Ensign, *February, 1988, pp.66-67*

Variations: *Establish how many miles it is to*

Grandpa's and then earn those miles as a family by doing chores, homework, having a good attitude around the house.

FAMILY TRIVIA GAME

Make a "Family Trivia" game. Questions for the game come from events in the lives of the parents and children. Question cards could contain categories and questions about family member's birthdays, anniversaries, schools attended, license plate numbers, favorite foods, special events, high school offices, family traditions, etc.

—Becky Bytheway Cooley, Salt Lake City, Utah

Variations: *Make up a trivia questionnaire and send it from family to family. Like the board game, serve each member a piece of pie as they answer a question correctly.*

MINUTES OF FAMILY EVENTS

Keep short minutes of family home evenings (who gives the prayers, who leads the song, what the activities were, the main point of the lesson and what everyone enjoyed as refreshments). They serve as a short review of the previous week's program and help to build self-esteem. Children love to hear their names read. Also record any event during the week that involved the family (an award, election, graduation, birth, death or birthday).

—Betty Lou Wintch, Tropic, Utah, Ensign, *June, 1982, p.73*

Variations: *These can also be recorded and the minutes can become a regular family journal. Copies can be included as part of letters to family members who are away.*

FAMILY IDEA FAIR

Within your ward, stake or neighborhood, sponsor an idea fair where members may share their own ideas for family fun, living on a budget, favorite foods, staying close and creating traditions.

—Melody Holland, Kailua, Hawaii

Variations: *You could even put together your own personalized idea book like this one. Try expanding and including ideas from your whole ward.*

FAMILY MEMORY BOARD

Every month, place a blank piece of poster board (22 x 14) on the wall of the family room or kitchen. Fill the board with family events, pictures, programs, news articles, etc. At the end of the month, retire the old board to the yearly collection and put up a new one. Then, every year, cover the posters with plastic and bind all twelve together with big rings.

—Susan Nord Green, Centerville, Utah, Ensign, *August, 1984, p.69*

Variations: *Keep a similar booklet for each child's best school work. Rather than using such large posters, try keeping the same things in a sticky-back photo album.*

REMEMBER WHEN?

Keep a small notebook handy and whenever something worth recording happens—something especially funny or tender—jot it down along with the date. Later, these experiences can be sorted and typed for personal histories. In the meantime, it's easy and can be pulled out and read over for some instant laughs.

—Leilani Hobgood Brandon, Salida, Colorado,
Ensign, *July, 1986, p.65*

FAMILY MISSIONARY BOARD

Many wards have a map of the world with strings pointing from certain areas to pictures and addresses of missionaries serving from the ward. Create a similar board in your home. In addition to posting the pictures and addresses of the missionaries in your ward, keep track of cousins, nephews, couples and family friends. Besides being a constant invitation to write to the missionary, it will provide a reminder of the importance of missions and allow you to honor those who take mission plans seriously before younger members of the family and visitors in your home.

—Chad and Beth Coons, Mesa, Arizona

Variations: *Put friends on the board as they earn their eagles, young womens' recognition award, Duty to God, etc. Place predictions on the board as to where different people might get called.*

FAMILY NIGHT PHANTOM

As you make your own refreshments, make a double batch and deliver it anonymously to another family in your ward. Perhaps the note attached could say something like this:

Family night is here again—time for stories and for fun.
Here's a special treat from us to eat together when you're done.
Next Monday it's your turn to make a treat—not once, but twice.
Then another family in our ward will have a snack that's nice.
The Family Night Phantom strikes again!

—*Janet Tucker, Ogden, Utah,*
Ensign, *January, 1980, p.66*

Variations: *Invite the family over and make the treat together. Rather than a treat, perform a service for the other family or present a skit or song that you have prepared. Challenge them to follow suit. Have members of your family fill out questionnaires on favorite foods, colors, music, sports, least favorite chore, etc. Then, draw names from a bowl. For one week, everyone arranges for secret surprises for the person whose name they drew (within your own family or in an exchange with another) using the questionnaire for ideas.*

—*Myrten and Vervene Grant, Lehi, Utah*

★ LOVE AND APPRECIATION

Pick a member of the family, and have each person complete the sentence "I love and appreciate ___________ because . . ." Go around the circle until everyone is finished. Pick a different person each week for home evening. A great way to give positive reinforcement!

★ FAMILY SALAD

Learn cooperation in a fun way by gathering in the kitchen and letting everyone help make a salad. It can be a fruit salad or a vegetable salad but everyone is in charge of an ingredient and gets to participate. Point out that, like each member of the family, each ingredient is different but makes the finished salad what it is.

—*Lory J. Holdaway, Henderson, Nevada,*
Ensign, *October, 1986, p.70*

Variations: *Also try pizza, stew, fondue, or a relish tray.*

VISUAL FAMILY STORIES

Make family history stories come alive by making them into flannel board stories or other visual aids. You can make transparent overlays, cards on craft sticks, flip charts, etc.

—Elaine C. Brewster, Salt Lake City, Utah, Ensign, *January, 1980, p.67*

Variations: *Try acting them out or writing them in short story form. Children can illustrate the stories or adults can draw simple pictures to go with each story that children can copy off and color as the story is being told or as a quiet activity in Church meetings.*

TRUE STORY TIME

Have the whole family dress for bed. Turn out all house lights and gather with pillows someplace where everyone can lie down. Announce the order of speakers, and then proceed to have each one tell any story they choose—with one condition: it must be a true story: from the scriptures, Church history, the experiences of General Authorities, our own lives or stories from family heritage. Everyone participates. Favorite stories are repeated often. It's also nice to end the day quietly.

—Jeanine Franson, Farmington, Maine, Ensign, *February, 1984, p.60*

Variations: *This is a chance to bear testimony to each other and learn points of the Gospel in an enjoyable way. Make picture book of true stories. Assemble a child's version of true stories from the lives of their grandparents and great-grand parents. Have an artist in the family or the children themselves illustrate each story. The volume can be reproduced and given to relatives for them to enjoy and learn from as well.*

—April Love, Spanish Fork, Utah, Ensign, *February, 1981, p.60*

FOOD FOR THOUGHT

School and sack lunches can be spiritually as well as nutritionally balanced. Sometimes when you include an apple or orange in the lunch, tape a spiritual thought to the fruit. Or write a short scripture on the napkin.

—*Michelle H. Cwiklinski, Cheedtowaga, New York,* Ensign, *Sept, 1981 p. 61*

Variations: *Place a thought, quote or scripture under pillows, in shoes, on a mirror or in a school book.*

★ GRAB BAGS

Every so often, exchange toys that your children have grown tired of with friends or family members who are in the same boat. Children get "new" toys without any expense. After all, one man's trash is another man's treasure.

—*Mary Lois Gunnell, Orem, Utah*

Variations: *Services, food, play clothes, books, tapes, etc.*

★ GRANDMA'S CLOSET

When giving gifts to lots of grandchildren, you might save a lot by giving some gifts that your grandchildren can enjoy in your home when they come to visit. A basket of toy animals kept at your home can be enjoyed by all your grandchildren and not just a few.

—*Caroline Eyring Miner, Salt Lake City, Utah,* Ensign, *August, 1986, pp.61-62*

Variations: *Collect favorite books they can read, dolls and balls, puzzles, board games, Church videos, etc.*

★ CHURCH MAGAZINES IN HOME EVENING

Each child is asked to give a synopsis of a story or article found in the magazine of his/her age group. Parents can present something from the Ensign. This is an excellent way for busy families to keep abreast of the Church magazines. If children forget and come unprepared, it becomes an excellent chance for everyone to listen together as someone reads a selected article and story from the magazine.

—*Charlene Higuera, Bakersfield, California,* Ensign, *January, 1984, p.68*

Variations: *Play a game to review main points of each article. Find out more about general authority authors. Copy pictures for younger children to color and or make into puzzles as they listen.*

THE JOURNAL CHAIR

For young children who can't yet write on their own, reserve a special place where they can take a turn sitting and remembering pleasant experiences they wish recorded. A parent or older brother or sister can act as a scribe and the child can fill empty places on the pages with his drawings or efforts at printing and spelling.

—*Fae Swinyard, Orem, Utah,* Ensign, *April, 1981, p.63*

Variations: *Fill a journal with special family memories, titling each incident. Invite brothers and sisters to all participate by including their fond memories too. This can be reproduced for the entire family.*

—*Diana B. Parker, Murray, Utah,* Ensign, *Sept, 1985, p.64*

LET'S DO LUNCH

Sometimes between busy work and Church schedules, time for parents and children to just be together and talk is hard to find. Try taking lunch time together. Go out, go home, or just meet at school. Most schedules provide a lunch break of some kind. See if you can't spend those breaks together.

—*Patty Fargo, Los Angeles, California,* Ensign, *August, 1986, p.62*

Variations: *Well . . . you could fast together.*

LET'S LOOK IT UP

At breakfast, offer children a challenge for the day. For the younger ones, perhaps a word to define. For the older ones, identifying the capitols of countries can be fun. Children know that those who have met the challenge by dinner get an extra big helping of dessert. This can make meal times, full of learning and interesting conversation for everyone.

—*Donna S. Moyer, Salt Lake City, Utah,* Ensign, *February, 1985, p.66*

Variations: *Look up scriptures or doctrinal questions. Challenge them to compliment a* *teacher, cafeteria working or janitor at school or work.*

Variations: *Make a college store or a Temple store.*

MONDAY NIGHT AT THE HOME MOVIES

Write a script or use a story like the Three Little Pigs and make a movie with your Video Recorder. Make costumes and use music. The finished movie will become a family treasure.

Variations: *Create a Family News broadcast, game show, scripture story, or "A day in the life of . . ." skit.*

MISSION STORE

Label a shoe box the "Mission Store" and put in it a supply of your children's favorite treats. When they want a goodie, rather than spending their allowances at the grocery store, they can come to you and the pennies, nickels, dimes and quarters are transferred into the children's own mission banks.

—*Karen Perkes, Bountiful, Utah,*
Ensign, *Oct, 1978, p.51*

REVERENCE CARDS

Before Church, fold several pieces of paper into shapes to make blank greeting cards. Then, during sacrament meeting, the children can quietly decorate the cards with drawings and stickers. During the next week, anonymously deliver the cards to families in the ward who need a cheery note.

—Ensign, *October, 1988, p.64*

Variations: *Make thank-you cards for teachers, Bishopric members, custodians, etc.*

SUNDAY SCRAPBOOKS

As an easy extension to your child's journal, provide a notebook in which they can mount anything brought home from Church. Preserve all the creative handouts and drawings that come home from Primary by slipping them into the scrapbook. You could even have the older children write about what they learned in Church. This will make the things that happen during Church meetings take on added meaning in the eyes of your children.

—Linda Wood Ballard, Pueblo, Colorado,
Ensign, *June, 1987, pp.66-67*

Variations: *Favorite scriptures, current scripture heroes, notes from classes, Sacrament meeting programs, etc.*

★ SCRIPTURE INTERNALIZING ACTIVITIES

Focus on characters or events in the scriptures and recreate similar circumstances for your children so that they have the opportunity to internalize the scriptures. An example would be to have a Nephi outing. Gather your children and put bandannas around all their heads. Tell them that you will have to leave your home and have them select what they feel will be the most necessary items. Go through a wilderness of some kind. You could include some brass plates that your children must return to your home to get. You could teach about the liahona as well. Analyze what main concepts you wish to focus on in any of the scripture stories and then set up similar situations that will help the story be more real in the minds of your children.

—Scott and Angel Anderson, Bluffdale, Utah

Variations: *Re-enact stories from Church history or the lives of Church leaders. Have your children create the circumstance for younger children or for friends.*

★ LIVE ON YOUR SEVENTY-TWO HOUR KIT

Select a weekend and live on your emergency supplies. You'll quickly realize what you need and don't need.

—Robin Gunnell, Debbie Hawkins, Orem, Utah

Variations: *Rotate the supplies in your kit at a predetermined interval such as every General Conference.*

★ SHRINKIES

Save the plastic lids of containers that come from the deli department of the grocery store. Draw pictures on them with permanent marker and them bake them in the oven at 500 degrees. The lids shrink to be no bigger than a half dollar. If you punch a hole in the top of the lid before baking it, they can be made into Christmas ornaments or play jewelry.

—Becky Crockett, Phoenix, Arizona

Variations: *The same thing can be done with styrofoam cups which shrink to resemble little hats [350 degrees for 30 seconds].*

A DAY TO BE SPECIAL

Every Sunday, draw slips of paper telling which day of the coming week will be their "special day." Each child gets one day a week to enjoy special privileges such as riding in the front seat of the car, running errands, helping Dad decide who is to say prayers, choose the story to be read at bedtime.

—Richard and Laua Daines, Hyde Park, Utah, Ensign, *April, 1983, p. 67*

Variation: *Let the selected child stay up longer than the rest of the family to get some undivided attention from mom and dad, including a love note and treat.*

STAR WATCH

Pull out an encyclopedia or a scout handbook and go to where you can see the stars. Find constellations, define light year and discuss the fact that some of the stars they are seeing might no longer exist. This can be a good time for spiritual discussions as well about God's creations, His power, and the degrees of glory.

—Jan Murphy, Tucson, Arizona, Ensign, *January, 1985, p.73*

Variations: *Make up your own constellations, name some of the stars after your own family. Try nature walks and learn the names of the trees and plants in your yard or at the Church.*

TOW WITH TOES

Have a contest to see what you can pick up with bare toes. It sounds peculiar, but you'll be amazed at the laughs you'll have as you practice toe dexterity. Try marbles, paper clips, spoons, pencils, etc.

—Jolene Richmond, Renton, Washington

Variations: *Use only your left hand, try things blind folded, draw with the pencil between your teeth or toes.*

★ NEW AND OLD TRADITIONS

Besides continuing your present family traditions, trace your family history back to discover from what countries your ancestors came. Then, adopt some of the native foods, costumes, and customs of those countries as part of your traditions. Holidays are an especially good time to focus on some of the places your family originally came from.

—Bonnie Jasperson, Heber City, Utah, Ensign, *December, 1986, p.55*

Variations: *Memorize facts about the country, learn traditional songs.*

★ TRAVELING LETTERS

A traveling letter is a packet of letters from each member of the family. It begins with the oldest member, who writes a letter and sends it to a younger brother or sister. This next family member then adds a letter and sends it on to the next person. This continues until the letter returns to the oldest, who removes his original letter, inserts a new one and starts the whole thing over again.

—Gaylin Rollins, Roy, Utah, Ensign, *July, 1984, p.68*

Variations: *The same idea could be incorporated to share thoughts, favorite scriptures or poems, etc.*

(Entry titles are shown in bold)

A

B

C

D

E

F

G

H

I

J

K

L

M

N

ACTIVITIES THAT TEACH

ARTS AND CRAFTS

CONFERENCES

DRAMA

FAMILY ACTIVITIES

FOOD

HERITAGE, FAMILY AND CHURCH

MINGLE ACTIVITIES

MISCELLANEOUS

MISSIONARY ACTIVITIES

MUSIC

SCRIPTURES

SERVICE

About the Authors

John Bytheway

Brad Wilcox

Mark Twain once said, "There ain't no surer way to find out whether you like people or hate them than to travel with them" (*Reader's Digest*, Jan, '90, p.144). If that is the test, John Bytheway and Brad Wilcox found out long ago that they were friends. They travel together all across the United States and Canada as they teach with such Church Education System programs as Especially For Youth, Education Days, Know Your Religion and BYU Outreach Youth Conferences. John and Brad love to be with the young people of the Church.

John introduces himself when he speaks by showing a Pictionary version of his name: an outhouse by a road—a "john by-the-way." He recently graduated from BYU in business and is pursuing a Master's degree in communications. Currently, he is the director of BYU Outreach Youth Conferences and the Best of Especially for Youth lecture series in the Marriott Center. John served his mission in the Philippines and is yet unmarried. His favorite pastimes include doing celebrity impersonations and running.

Brad is a teacher. He is currently on the faculty in the College of Education at BYU. Brad served his mission in Chile and he and his wife, Debi, have three children. One of the funniest things he has done recently was winning with his in-laws on *Family Feud.*

Both John and Brad enjoy music and have sung on LDS tapes. They also found out that they are distantly related through a common ancestor who came to this continent on the Mayflower. Perhaps that is why they both love Twix candy bars and pepperoni pizza.